"I appreciate Larson's ...es simply, clearly, and without jargon. This is tremendously ...e information for the creative sector. Larson demystifies finance and and helps non-finanical people to make well-informed decisions."
  Mary-Kim Arnold, Executive Director
  Rhode Island Council for the Humanities

"Larson is that rare combination of artist and finance guru. As part of his ongoing work as an arts advocate, Larson has crafted a book that will appeal to anyone interested in learning the basics of personal finance through more creative means. The "Key Terms" at the back of the book alone make it a wonderful resource. The stories and illustrations will help finance-phobes and novices learn to manage their money in simple and effective ways."
  Cristina M. DiChiera, Director of Artists Programs
  Rhode Island State Council on the Arts

"My clientele includes many wonderful artists who desperately want to succeed financially -- but no one talks to them in a way they can understand...*Peace, Love, and Financial Planning* is a gift from the Gods, via Larson Gunness. The books is funny and the case -studies are right-on. The illustrations and easy writing style make the information even more digestible...Larson is a smart financial planner, but what sets him apart is his ability to create stories that speak to people. His artistic background and his humanity shine through. And don't miss the Glossary! It's a hoot!"
  Richard Streitfeld, CPA, CFE
  Aaronson, Lavoie Streitfeld Diaz and Co, PC

"Larson's book provides an accessible and humorous window into the real world, nitty gritty details of financial planning: the details that many of my estate planning clients nod in agreement with when we meet, yet don't really have a handle on. Everyone should go through the exercise of the financial statement and the reality of a working budget."
  W. Parish Lentz; Davis & Lentz, LLC

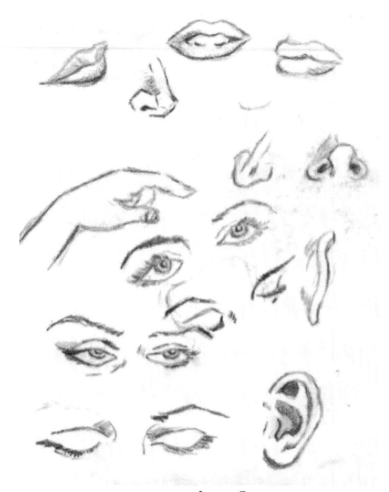

Larson Gunness

Peace, Love, and Financial Planning
an illustrated guide to money

by

E. Larson Gunness

ISBN:0985257601
ISBN-13: 978-0985257606

Published by GFS in 2012 in Barrington, RI

www.peaceloveandfinancialplanning.org

ABOUT THE AUTHOR

E. Larson Gunness in a creative entrepreneur who lives in Barrington, RI with his wife and two children. The Peace, Love, and Financial Planning project brings together the two halves of his brain by blending his creative practice with his professional skills in the field of personal finance.

In his business career, he has over 14 years of experience in the financial sector (with Smith Barney, Fidelity Investments, and since 2006 at the helm of his own firm). He went to B-school at MIT Sloan and went to Kenyon College for his undergraduate degree in Economics.

Also, he has developed a creative practice as a musician, writer, and visual artist. He earned an MFA in Interdisciplinary Arts from Goddard College. He has taught financial literacy to artists for several years now.

From 1989—1991 he was a Peace Corps Volunteer in the Dominican Republic (a tough job he did indeed love). He was writer, editor, and subject matter expert (financial planning) for this book and the related website of the same name (peaceloveandfinancialplanning.org). He illustrated the chapter titled "The Alchemy of Investing."

"Artists listen to me," he says, "because I am one of them."

DEDICATIONS AND ACKNOWLEDGEMENTS

I dedicate this to all the creative souls out there: yours is important work. And of course I dedicate this to my family, without whom I'd be alone.

I owe many thanks to all of the good people who helped me incubate and grow this project. I approached this work as a collaborative art project and, as such, owe a great debt to the experts, from both the arts and the professions, who each helped shape this by adding their voice: Don Morton and his team at RISD of Natalie and Rachel were so vital to me in my early stages; the state arts agency RISCA, I couldn't thank Cristina DiChiera enough for her openness and insights; to each of the illustrators: it was a delight to see how you interpreted the characters, Jim Bush, Allison Boesch, Ivy Tai, Anna Rosenfeld, Elizabeth Cole Sheehan, and Jeff Cooperman, your work is ingenious; I'd also like to thank my regular *Creatives Group* of Robert Leaver, Stan DAngelis, Brian Fielding, Nora Hall, and of course Pete Hocking (Pete, I have to give you particular thanks for all of your brilliance and mentorship); I'd like to thank Jorge Paricio and his keen eye for design; I want to thank all of the wonderful and hardworking arts organizations here in RI that allowed me to learn and teach with them: New Urban Arts, Steelyard, Craftland, AS220, RISD Quickies, RI CItizens for the Arts, and the Arts and Cultural Alliance of Newport County; many thanks to my professional collaborators Rich Streitfeld, Gio Cicione, and Parish Lentz; and finally, thanks to Liana, Jamie, and Maria, who respectively have the wisdom and courage of Athena, Percy, and Annabeth.

CONTENTS

This page intentionally left blank, because I needed to format things correctly and, since you're a creative, your brain may already have begun to wander...so don't put this book down, doodle on this page, then keep on reading. Thanks and peace!

INTRODUCTION

Money. Finance. Budgeting. Planning. These words are boring, wicked boring.

Fact is, you don't like money, don't want to even deal with it. You have more important and compelling things to do with your life force. You are a creative soul. You focus your mind on that which is beautiful and true. Money is not beautiful...money is crass and gaudy, the root of all evil. You'd just as soon not even know a thing about it.

But, alas, there's no way around it. No simple and pure route. There are some things you just have to know. Money is one of those things.

You'd be willing to learn if you could just find the right material, an approach that actually held your attention. Boring textbooks, seminars, webinars, blogs, talking heads, and websites just don't cut it for you.

And money was not part of your curriculum back when you were in school. It's not that you're not smart enough. You know you can learn. You just need to find the right teachers. You need to find people who understand you and can speak your language.

But wait! There's hope! What if you could learn from other creatives?

Welcome.

This book has been developed by creatives (of many genres) for creatives (of any genre). Because we know what you deal with (at least some of it!). We are certain that you have all the brain power and discipline you'll ever need to manage the financial side to your life. You're rigorous in other areas of your life, right? Like your creative practice? Or your avocations? This shouldn't be any different.

All you lack is some training (okay, you may lack interest, but that's another issue...). It really won't take much for you to become comfortable in your own personal finances. You can, and should, be the boss of your own money. Read on. We hope our work here helps you.

Jim Bush

SO HOW DO WE PROPOSE TO TEACH THIS TOPIC?

Instead of droning on and on about terms and concepts, we take a different approach: we tell stories. Everyone loves stories.

Using a combination of stories, a glossary of terms, lovely illustrations (by cool creatives, just like you), and even some graphs and tables (don't worry), we present the major concepts you need to know about money. No, we can't make you an expert. But hopefully we can help demystify money. Hopefully you'll find a way to think about money that gives you clarity and confidence.

The stories in this book (called "case studies" if you want to get all pedagogical about it), are based on true life stories—of course the names and places have been changed to protect the ignorant. We've talked to enough people in tough situations (heck we've *been* people in tough situations) that we feel qualified to tell stories about the financial and business trouble that creatives often face.

In reading and thinking about how other creatives face and deal with various problems, you can learn about how to deal with your own challenges. We bet you'll see yourself in these stories.

Jeff Cooperman

WHAT WE COVER IN THE FOLLOWING PAGES:

Chapter One: Mortgages 101; All of the Sudden, It's Complicated - Syd and Nanci find things get complicated quickly. They need to face facts and get organized as they go through the mortgage process. *(Illustrations by Jim Bush)*

Chapter Two: Financial Statements; Let's Get It Together - Syd and Nanci learn the basic worksheets they need in order to get organized. *(Illustrations by Ivy Tai)*

Chapter Three: Paying Your Taxes; It's Not Your Money - Art learns the hard way about how to pay taxes, work with a CPA, and what not to do. *(Illustrations by Anna Rosenfeld)*

Chapter Four: Getting a Grant; The Grant Rant - Art, Syd, and Nanci reveal their true selves through their different approaches to seeking grant funding for projects. *(Illustrations by Jeffrey Cooperman)*

Chapter Five: Debt; Yeehah! Free Money! Prudence devises the perfect, foolproof method of managing debt. Then life intervenes. *(Illustrations by Elizabeth Cole Sheehan)*

Chapter Six: Are Artist Co-Ops a Good Idea? Art School Afterlife - A bunch of good friends live together, share expenses, share studio space. *(Illustrations by Allison Boesch)*

Chapter Seven: The Dark Alchemy of Investing - Beware all who enter this land. *(Illustrations by E. Larson Gunness)*

Glossary - You know you should know this stuff, but never found the right place to learn it.

CHAPTERS ARE EACH ORGANIZED THE SAME WAY

Key Chapter Concepts - What are the key topics covered?

Case Study - Like all stories, our cases could prompt many different discussions. But each is primarily focused on a narrow scope of financial topics. The stories present issues and challenges. They make us think.

Questions to Talk About - Maybe you'll want to wrestle with some questions. You could talk about them, you could journal, you could write poetry or songs. Whatever helps you learn.

Just Tell Me How - You might want to zero in on how to apply this information to your actual life. This section is hands—on, to tell you what to do and how. So if you're in a big rush, or just can't be bothered with story time, then just go directly to this section. But you won't have as much fun.

Key Terms - As fun and artsy as we try to make this subject, at some point, you'll just have to learn some terms and concepts. The final section of each chapter includes a list of things mentioned in the chapter that might need an explanation. Also, at the back of the book is an alphabetized glossary that includes the terms and concepts from each chapter.

Illustrations - And of course, there are graphics. Several illustrators (including the author) contributed artwork to this book. We think the illustrations make the book more fun to look at and learn from; much more fun than just text and numbers, text and numbers, text and numbers. Don't you agree?

AND YOUR GUIDES FOR THIS LEARNING ADVENTURE?

Now, you didn't think we'd send you off into the world of finance all on your own, did you? We give you Syd and Nanci (get the joke?), and Art, Prudence, and Nunzio. These are the lyric souls who serve as your guides.

SYD

He's a ceramicist, puppeteer, and everyone's friend. What's not to like? He is easy to get along with; doesn't make waves. Prefers to go along to get along. Plus, he's seldom ever awake during daylight hours, he does all his work at night. And

whenever he is up during the day, he's too groggy to do much more than smile and sip at his coffee.

Jim Bush

NANCI

Nanci works hard. At first she wasn't certain that she even belonged at art school. But, after persevering through all of the ups and downs, she found her niche and established herself as a painter who demonstrates great intelligence and potential. She's also a pretty kickin' bass player and wants to start a band one day... She doesn't have all

the answers all the time; but she listens to what others say, watches what goes on around her, and generally tries to do the right thing.

Ivy Tai

ART

Art is a prodigy. Even in a community full of talented people, his work stands out. He is known around campus as the most naturally gifted classical painter of his cadre. He produces amazing work, seemingly without effort. He's wildly prolific, and his studio would be filled with his paintings, if they weren't so sought after by gallery owners from New York to LA. But

he's hard to be close to because, though he's sweet as can be when he's sober, he's rarely sober. He pursues the life of the debauched artist with all the energy and intensity that his peers reserve for their creative work.

Anna Rosenfeld

PRUDENCE

She's an illustrator of the highest caliber. Her work is intricate and precise, and she does not let it out of her hands before it is finished, *completely* finished, to a level that meets her superlative standard for perfection. Problem is, her standards are so high that she has trouble ever feeling like any of her work is ever completely "ready."

Elizabeth Cole

NUNZIO

And then there's Nunzio. Nunzio is rich, handsome, cultured, and lazy. He is, in actual fact, European royalty (from some unrecognizable nation state in Western Europe). At different times during his undergraduate work, he's been a painter, architect, illustrator, graphic artist, sculptor, and poet. None seemed to stick. Or maybe they all have. And, as he explains, "Though each genre offered a window, none was quite large enough for my heart to shine through." So he simply refers to himself as an artist, and leaves it at that. He's quite friendly and attentive, but he often disappears for days on end. After these absences, he'll return, his tan noticeably deeper, wearing expensive new shoes or top coat or satchel.

Allison Boesch

CHAPTER ONE - MORTGAGES 101

> **Key Chapter Concepts:**
> - No denial!
> - Avoidance is expensive.
> - Overview of the mortgage process.

Case Study: All of the Sudden, It's Complicated

Once upon a time, there were two artists: a musician/painter and a puppeteer, who found that their once carefree lives had become complex, very very complex.

Let's meet Syd and Nanci...

For the first time since graduating from a prestigious New England design school, they rent space in a house over on the West Side of Providence, Rhode Island. It's a neighborhood where a number of their friends live—quirky vintage homes and a diversity of small businesses such as auto repair, check cashing, pawn brokerage, and the tattoo arts.

Moving into an actual house was a step up in the world for Syd and Nanci. Prior to this move, they'd lived in a Westfalia that Nanci had inherited from her favorite uncle. And though the van had served them well for many years, when Syd parked it on

the day of the move, it shuddered and slumped, as though heaving a sigh of relief that its travels were finally done and it was home to stay. No longer tasked with travel, the van's sole remaining function became late night office space where Syd and his friends *collaborate*.

During the early stages of their careers, things were simple. Expenses were low, apart from buying gas and paying for occasional repairs. Had it not been for the Westfalia's lack of a full bathroom, they might be living there still. Or Syd might. For her part, Nanci never adjusted to a rarely bathed vanmate.

"I couldn't build up a tolerance," she explained. "And now that we're in an apartment, he thinks it's the move that rekindled our romance. I suppose that's accurate enough."

Nanci plays bass for a punk band named "Mick's My Mother" (a band that groupies refer to as "M-cubed") and she wrote the band's song: "I Don't Like You." They only have the one song; but one's been enough. It's a sixty-minute romp that evolves and changes with each successive set. Fans don't care about the lack of variety, don't even seem to notice. Every show is packed and, from the moment Nanci's bass starts pounding, the riot is on.

Nanci is also the band leader. She handles business aspects such as booking, promotion, and scheduling rehearsals. In the early days, promotion was all by word of mouth and band management involved just making sure the instruments arrived intact and the leather didn't mildew.

In recent years, as the band has become increasingly successful, Nanci had to take on additional activities. For example, a club owner who regularly books her act recently introduced her to a graphic design firm to discuss signage. Up to this point, all the band's posters and other collateral had been handled by a loose collection of friends from art school, who were generally payable in-kind with either beer, comp tickets to shows, or some combination of both. Working with an actual design firm was a new experience for her, and did not clearly (in her opinion) produce superior results.

In return for her efforts she receives half of the band's earnings. On average, she takes home some cash each month from various band activities such as revenue from gigs, CD and

MP3 sales, and merchandising (the pre-ripped and lightly soiled concert tee shirt is ever popular, as are reprinted posters from previous shows).

Syd describes himself as "a brick puppeteer performance artist for solo shows." This means that he has developed a creative practice in which he uses bricks as puppets in intimate two-hour performances for only a sole audience member—that's right, one person, in the audience.

"The intimacy," he claims "is vital for the stories I tell."

Though he has grand plans, he has only just begun to attract attention for his shows. So, to earn money to pay his share of rent and for supplies such as bricks, costumes, and jewelry (Syd wears the costumes and jewelry, the puppets perform nude), he works at a local fast food hamburger chain.

He claims he "doesn't enjoy working with meat" but seems to like the dress up aspect of the job—he assumes a rakish and ironic demeanor whenever he is in uniform.

He brings home a small salary each week, after tax. He also receives benefits such as a **401k** in which he contributes $5 per month.

Times of Smooth Sailing...

Leaving the road for the stability of a second floor apartment was a step that they did not take lightly. Syd cried himself to sleep for the first three nights they were "on the inside" until Nanci got wise to him, hid away his NyQuil, and agreed to read him a bedtime story each night until he got himself settled.

Everything seemed stable over in West Providence. Their combined income was enough to cover rent, food, and supplies. M-cubed continued to draw big crowds at every show. A more rested and cleaner Syd began to actually book performances. There wasn't exactly a flurry of interest, but enough that he began to consider whether he should cut back his hours at the restaurant.

What was more, some old friends from college, started renting out the first floor of the house. They were artists too, but also had jobs as primary school teachers in order to make ends meet. From Nanci's perspective, it was good to have friends under the same roof, made the place seem like a home.

Things went on like this for almost a year. Went so smoothly that Nanci caught herself occasionally wondering whether she might one day heed the call from her biological clock (a call that had become unmistakably loud of late) and consider whether and how to bring a baby into their lives.

She of course never told Syd about these notions—not because she worried whether he'd want a baby. He would. It was more that she just didn't want to deal with the sappy glomming he would no doubt subject her to at the idea of shared parenthood.

Then, over the course of a month, things changed.

Winds of Change

The changes began with a call from the landlord. Syd took the call, listening absently while the landlord explained he'd decided to sell the house. The landlord told Syd to make sure to tell this news to Nanci. Then hung up.

Syd thought about this news for a time...about four-seconds. Then he went to his studio, not giving it another thought for several days when finally, he mentioned it to Nanci one evening before she left for rehearsal.

Appalled that it had taken him so long to give her the message, she stood before him for several minutes, screaming. There were so many things about his lapse that angered her, she wasn't quite sure what she'd yelled at him and what she held back. As she walked the half mile to the band's rehearsal space, she calmed down. Surely this was something she could talk the landlord out of. Or they could find some alternative solution. She could handle it.

Next day at noon, she called the landlord. It didn't take long to establish that the situation was indeed quite grave. The landlord explained he was overextended on his various businesses. For this particular property, he'd taken on an **ARM** loan, which had recently adjusted to a higher rate. At the higher rate, he could no longer meet his payments. He said he was thinking about negotiating a **short sale** arrangement with his bank, which meant he'd need to move quickly. Rather than raise rent to cover payments, he'd decided to just take a loss on the property and reduce his overall debt load.

Nanci was shocked. After several minutes of discussion, she was able to get him to at least give her an informal agreement to make an offer on the house. She decided that was the best she could do, given the circumstances. So she thanked him for offering some hope, and hung up.

She knew what she was going to do: she was going to buy this property, live in it and rent the other floors out to her artsy friends. But that meant a **mortgage**. And Nanci didn't know the first thing about getting a mortgage.

Syd took the landlord's news as an "invasion of his personal sovereignty." A reaction which, though it in no way surprised Nanci, struck her as endlessly counterproductive. But what could she do? Syd was Syd.

He responded in several ways. After three days swinging between bouts of dramatic crying and furious phone calls to everyone he'd ever known to tell them he loved them "before it was too late," he finally settled in on a self-constructed "detoxification and salvation" regimen consisting of raw foods, green tea, orally consumed marijuana, and Tibetan prayer.

Holding no great allegiance to the tools of western psychiatric care, Nanci was happy to have Syd follow his alternative pathway. Just to be safe, she made sure he went to bed early every night, thinking that at least a rested distraught and medicated Syd would be preferable to an exhausted one.

Luckily, that night was not a performance night for either Nanci or Syd. They had time to talk. Nanci caught Syd just before he was about to settle in on one of his four-hour self-healing sessions.

"We need to talk about all of this," she said to him. "We need to focus."

Questions to think about:

1. Did things really turn complicated all of the sudden?

2. How could Syd and Nanci have been better prepared?

3. Do you think that maybe people like these just aren't the types who will ever be well prepared? Will they always be in crisis mode?

4. What should they do?

5. Would your suggestions resolve all of their problems or just one or two of them?

JUST TELL ME HOW

Let's pretend Syd and Nanci came to you for advice. They told you about their situation with the landlord, and that they want to buy the house. What would you have them do? You can't do much of anything on their behalf, right? But you can help them think through the steps they'll have to take.

They may face many challenges, but let's focus on just two of them:

> 1. Syd is in denial.
> 2. They need to learn about mortgages.

Syd's in Denial

The point is that times can get tough. So face them. Avoidance is expensive! That's why this is the first chapter in this book. Times will get tough, and messy, and confusing. So what do many of us do when times get tough? We ignore. Slip comfortably into denial. Avoid facing facts.

Because who wants to deal with all that difficult, inextricable, uncorrectable stuff? It's much easier to just deny and avoid. For a little while. But before too long of course, it will all catch up with you. Even when there are no obvious solutions out there, you do yourself no favors by avoiding problems. You'll only make things worse. Avoidance is expensive!

Nanci seems like she's decided to start facing things, right? Great for her! Doesn't mean things get easier for her overnight, just means that she now has a fighting chance of eventually getting things straightened out.

If you were going to advise Syd and Nanci to begin to face it, how would you suggest they go about doing that?

They should begin talking about their financial problems. They should talk with each other, with people who care about them (like friends and family), maybe they should talk with someone who has experience dealing with the specific problem they face.

After talking for a bit, they could make lists of things like what they know, what they need to learn, and what needs to be done when. They need to clarify the problems they face and identify how to respond. No need to be high tech, just be active.

The point is, stop avoiding the issue. In Syd and Nanci's case, they need to learn whether or not they can buy the house from the landlord. This will require a mortgage. Have either of them ever had a mortgage? Do they know what the steps involved are?

How to Get a Mortgage

If the landlord is having financial problems, then he may be in a rush to unload the property (sometimes it seems like everyone's struggling, doesn't it?). For an entrepreneurial person like Nanci, this situation could provide a great opportunity. Could be a perfect chance to buy the house.

If they decide to try to buy the house, it would make sense for them to seek help from a real estate agent, who can walk them through this process. At the very least, they'll need a lawyer who deals with real estate transactions. It just wouldn't be wise for them to try to do this on their own. Artists are great do-it-yourselfers. Nonetheless, it's important to know when to look for (and pay for) help. This is one of those times.

Even still, Syd and Nanci will have to be active participants in the process and need to educate themselves about how this whole buying a house thing works.

If this deal goes the way of the short sale, Syd and Nanci may well get a great bargain. If this becomes a more standard real estate transaction, the realtor will be very helpful in seeing Syd and Nanci through the process. The realtor will make sure that they don't overlook critical steps (such as doing a title search and setting up an appraisal).

The Mortgage Process

It takes about a month to six weeks to get through the whole mortgage process, assuming there aren't any snags. There are a bazillion forms and documents to be signed (which didn't, incidentally, prevent the catastrophe of the 2008-2009 collapse...). In essence, there are three stages to the process: there's the application, underwriting, and closing. Assuming Syd and Nanci know the value (price) of the house, they'll need to come up a down payment.

Down Payment - 100% financing! (in other words, making no down payment) is sometimes advertised by sellers and lenders. This is a bad idea. If Syd and Nanci buy a house and put no money down, and the house drops in value, then they owe more than the house is worth. This is called being "underwater." They should not do this. Syd and Nanci need to make sure they have a way to come up with cash that can be put toward a down payment. First time homebuyers sometimes get this cash from savings, from selling some other assets, or through some arrangement with family members. A good threshold for a down payment is 20%. If they can put 20% or more toward the house, then they'll avoid additional costs on their mortgage.

Application - Potential borrowers can go through the application process with a mortgage firm, online, at a big multinational bank, or through other form of lender. It'd be best for Syd and Nanci to go to a physical bank, like a local branch office in or near their neighborhood. Smaller banks and **credit unions** can often be more customer friendly than the big behemoth banks, and can offer the same exact mortgage products.

The application stage is where Syd and Nanci fill out forms and provide all sorts of information such as sources of income, prior year tax returns, any assets they own, outstanding debt, and personal identification information like a driver's license or passport. The bank will also seek Syd and Nanci's written permission to look up their **credit scores**. See the Key Concepts section for more on credit scores, but for now you should just understand that credit scores are the information infrastructure developed by the financial industry to evaluate how reliable a person might be when it comes to repaying a loan.

Also, at an early point in the application process, the bank will offer Syd and Nanci the opportunity to *lock in* an interest rate. Since interest rates can move up or down according to the mercurial whim of the global economy, locking in means that from that point forward, the interest rate for that specific loan will not move, throughout the process. What has happened here is that the bank has found a specific lender out there who, based on the preliminary information Syd and Nanci have provided, is willing to offer a loan under the terms presented, at a specific rate. Locking in a rate is good for both the lender and for Syd and Nanci, because it just wouldn't make anyone comfortable to have the rate fluctuating all the way until the final day of the signing. It's better if everyone can decide on the rate that they're willing to accept, then move forward from there.

Appraisal - During the application stage, an appraisal will be done on the property in question. Syd and Nanci should feel encouraged when the bank sends out the appraiser; it means that the application has successfully progressed to an advanced stage. The lender will hire their own appraiser and make Syd and Nanci pay for it. If this sounds a bit odd, it really isn't. The appraiser is going to go to the house and look it over, inside and out. They'll walk around with a clipboard and camera, jotting down notes and taking snapshots of bathrooms and the kitchen. They also look around the outside and at the roof. Finally, they look at "comparables" which are houses in the same neighborhood that are, as close as possible, similar to the one Syd and Nanci want to buy. Comparables are never a perfect match (unless you're talking about some cookie-cutter subdivision, of which there are thousands in these United States).

The appraiser also looks at the trend in house prices in the neighborhood: are they going up? Falling? And what's the socioeconomic makeup of the neighborhood. This stage can seem messy from a social justice perspective, because lenders are making and acting upon judgements about the financial health of neighborhoods....

Once the appraiser's information has been gathered, the lender feels they can evaluate the relative value of the house. Don't forget, this house is **collateral** behind the mortgage—meaning that if Syd and Nanci stopped paying, the bank owns the house.

Underwriting - If all goes well during the application process, that is, if Syd and Nanci can provide the lender with all the information it asks for, in an acceptable format (not always as easy as it sounds), the lender begins the underwriting process. The underwriter goes through the information provided in the application with a fine toothed comb, verifying the accuracy and soundness of the application.

The underwriter might seek to verify some areas (such as employment) and look for additional supporting information in others (such as seeking a letter from the accountant that does the books for Nanci's band, to verify her income). While it might feel intrusive to Syd and Nanci for the underwriting department to ask so many questions, it's not so unreasonable if you look at it from the lender's perspective. The lender is in the process of giving a big amount of money to two people that they've never physically met. It seems only fair that they get to learn about the people they're being asked to lend to. Of course, banks have certainly done ill deeds in the past (go online and look up "red lining" or "toxic assets"), but for the most part when the process works, the underwriting stage gives lenders a chance to understand the risk they will undertake when they lend money.

Closing - After all the information provided during the application process is examined and considered closely (during underwriting), the next step is to close the sale. Syd and Nanci only make it this far if they've satisfied everything everything everything in the eyes of the lender. Under normal circumstances, the closing is attended by the prior owner, the lender, the buyer, and often a realtor or two, if they were involved in the process. If people can't attend in person, sometimes it is acceptable to send an authorized representative.

During the actual closing meeting, the property is formally transferred from one owner to another. Papers are completed and signed. Keys are turned over. The deed is legally transferred. Syd and Nanci may have to present a certified check to cover closing costs. Closing costs can include items like the appraiser's fee, title fee, credit report fee, lawyer's fee (for title search and such). Also, it may be necessary to include a portion of the insurance and taxes into the closing costs as well. In all, closing costs could be a couple of thousand dollars.

KEY TERMS

ARM - With an Adjustable Rate Mortgage the rate you'd pay will change (or "adjust") over the term of the loan. Do you think it will adjust *down*? Hah! See Mortgages, Variable for more.

Collateral - When a loan is secured by collateral, that means the lender will own the collateral if the borrower defaults. A house is the collateral on a mortgage. A car is the collateral on an auto loan. Unsecured loans have no collateral. Examples of this are credit cards, department store cards, or other forms of consumer debt. Since there is no collateral for the lender to seize if the borrower defaults, then the interest rates are usually higher.

Credit Scores and Credit Rating - (See subsequent chapter on Debt) In order for a potential lender to decide whether you'll pay them back, a system of evaluating your creditworthiness has developed over the years. Creditworthiness is essentially concerned with how good someone is at paying off their loans on time and in full. Most people in the US, sometime during their late teenage years to early twenties, began to establish evidence of their creditworthiness (called a credit history). You, without even knowing it, have left behind you a trail of evidence as to your creditworthiness.

There are three bureaus that gather and compile this type of information. These three bureaus are Equifax, Experian, and TransUnion. Then, the Fair Isaac Corporation uses this info to create a number that lenders (such as banks, credit card issuers and the like) use to evaluate your credit risk. This score is called your FICO score.

There are several things that matter in your credit score (or your FICO score). According to the myFICO.com website, 35%

of your score is from your payment history (on things like rent, debt payments, cell phone payments), 30% is how much you owe, 15% is the length of your credit history, 10% is the amount of new credit, and 10% is the types of credit used. Remember credit means the same thing as loans or debt.

Credit Unions - These act like small local banks, but are actually a different form of financial institution. Usually, they serve a small neighborhood or community of people. The important point here is that credit unions are more in the retail consumer business. That means they are more interested in individual customers (like you and me), as opposed to the mega-banks, who only really want to do business with other mega-corporations or with gazillionaires.

Debit Card - These are often confused with credit cards, but they behave differently. Many bank accounts (or other accounts where someone holds money) offer debit cards as a way to get money out of the account. When you purchase something with a debit card, the process looks and feels similar to using a credit card. You swipe your card and, instead of signing your name, you sometimes have to enter your PIN code. From then on, the item you purchased is yours.

Except what happens behind the scenes is different from credit. With a debit card, the amount of your transaction is deducted from your bank account. So if you buy something for $45 and you used you debit card, shortly after your transaction at the cashier or checkout (again, real or virtual), your account is reduced, or debited, $45.

This is handy because you don't have to carry around cash. And, you aren't charged interest because you're not taking a loan as with a credit card.

Though debit cards can be a great tool, there are two main problems with them, problems that aren't often talked about. First, there are fees that can arise that you might not know about (such as transaction fees, annual fees and getting whacked if you overdraw your account). The second problem is that people generally spend more when they use debit cards—a lot more. Retailers and banks know this. They're very good at separating you from your money. Carry cash and use that.

Mortgages, Fixed Rate - Most people don't have enough cash laying around that they can buy a house outright, so they put some money down (hopefully more than 20%) and borrow the rest. The money they borrow is called a mortgage. In a fixed rate mortgage, the rate of interest you pay to the lender never changes, throughout the length (or term) of the loan (or mortgage). For example, if you had a 30 year, fixed rate mortgage, your interest rate wouldn't change on that mortgage for 30 years. This can be helpful in terms of planning, because you'll know exactly what you owe, each month, for thirty years. You can pay mortgages off early, but if you don't, you know what you'll owe. Typical terms for fixed rate mortgages are 15, 20, and 30 years.

Mortgages, Variable Rate - Like the definition above, except in this case the interest rate can change over the life of the loan. For example, some variable rate mortgages have a super duper low rate which doesn't change for a certain period, like 5 years. Then, once that 5 years is up, the rate is adjusted. Upwards. Becoming much more expensive. These types of mortgages can be good if you were only planning to own a certain property for a couple of years (some people move a lot). But if you were planning to live in a certain property for many years, think hard about the adjusting rate feature before signing on for a variable rate mortgage. It might be a fit for you, but then again, it might not.

Short Sale - A short sale is process undertaken by 1.) a person who owns a property that is worth less that the mortgage, 2.) the lender who provided that mortgage, and 3.) a potential buyer of the property. There may also be real estate lawyers or short sale consultants involved to negotiate the terms of the transaction. Short sales are negotiated and executed on a case by case basis - the outcome is certain until all parties agree and the deal is done.

There are many resources a person could turn to in order to learn about short sales. The FDIC, Freddie Mac, Fannie Mae, and state housing agencies all have educational resources available. Also, banks often provide resources, but be careful because banks are in the business of selling mortgages and other financial services. You have to understand that just about everyone in the financial services world is marketing themselves in one way or another, so be aware.

Sometimes, especially during the housing crisis that began in 2007 or so, borrowers can get over their heads with their debt obligations and become simply unable to pay back their loans. A short sale can be a way out of this mess. The lender or bank will be willing to consider a short sale application only as a last resort before foreclosure.

For a lender, a short sale is making the best of a bad situation: either the lender accepts a short sale, or the homeowner completely walks away from the mortgage (that is, stops paying, permanently) and the bank is stuck owning a vacant house. The short sale can be a slightly better (though still bad) solution.

So if this unhappy situation arises, the borrower (homeowner) may contact the lender and explain how they just cannot afford to pay anymore. The lender may decide to begin the short sale application process.

Unsolicited editorializing: Let's just remember bankers are the ones who created and pushed through these inappropriate mortgages in the first place. In this author's humble opinion, the scale of blame tips decidedly toward the financial industry, who made a helluva living off of selling mortgages, mortgages, mortgages.

401k - The 401k is a retirement plan arrangement that was developed by the IRS to encourage Americans to save their own money for their own retirement. Conceptually, these plans really favor the individual account owner and can be a very good thing. Plans are sponsored (or set up) by an employer for employees. Each employee who wants to participate (i.e., become a "participant," clever, huh?) can open an account in the 401k plan. They can contribute a certain amount from their periodic pay into their 401k account. Within their account, they can usually invest in a variety of different mutual funds, sometimes also in company stock.

Contributions that are made by the employee are tax deductible. So, say an employee pays taxes on $30,000 income per year. If they contribute $3,000 to their 401k plan, then they'd reduce the amount of taxable income by the amount of their contribution, to $27,000. There are limits to how much an employee can contribute per year, but those limits are relatively high, like $16,500 per person for 2011.

The contributions grow and cannot be accessed (without penalty) until the account owner reaches the age of 59.5 (why the half year? Ask congress). Some time after that age is reached, when the account owner starts to take distributions, they will pay income taxes on what they take out, at their then current tax rate. If they wait until they are 70.5 before taking distributions, the IRS will make them begin to take required distributions each year. The amount of the required distribution is governed by a table published by the IRS each year.

If someone takes money out of their retirement account before they are 59.5, they will have to pay income taxes on the amount of the distribution, plus they'll pay a 10% penalty. So, for every dollar withdrawn before age 59.5, a person could end up only seeing 65% of that.

CHAPTER TWO - FINANCIAL STATEMENTS

> **Key Chapter Concepts:**
> 1. Time to get organized.
> 2. How to create and use basic financial statements.

Case Study: Get it Together

Your old friends, Syd and Nanci, reached out to you because they are in financial disarray. Nanci called one day and explained how her records are a mess, a complete mess. She has lost confidence about where she is financially. She doesn't know with any certainty whether or not there will be enough cash in her account to cover expenses. And Syd, sweet serene Syd, is no help at all because he claims he doesn't even believe in money. What's she supposed to do with that? They can't live on the edge any more. It's time. They need to get organized.

You tell her to relax, that you have been learning a lot about money lately. You have found some great educational resources for artists who want to learn about this stuff. You feel you can help. You tell her you'll be right over.

When you arrive, you knock on the front door;

you know to knock loudly because the doorbell doesn't work. Someone must have been waiting because immediately you are buzzed in. You climb the narrow stairs of their newly-purchased house (they live upstairs, and rent out the lower floors) and push your way through the partially open door to their apartment. As you pass through the cluttered and dusty front room, a black cat blinks at you from its perch on a windowsill. The cat appears cross with you for disturbing its nap, and you feel a bit guilty.

You find Syd and Nanci in the kitchen. They are seated across from each other at the kitchen table: a chipped but serviceable, 1950s-era, yard sale special. Syd sits low, in a chair more suited for a den than kitchen. Nanci's chair is of a more standard kitchen variety, but not a set that matches the table.

The way they are seated makes Syd look like a small child and Nanci like the weary adult charged with his custody.

On the table between them is a wrinkled and stained grocery bag, filled with scores of receipts and scraps of paper. They turn anxious faces toward you as you enter. Syd tilts the bag toward you and bits of paper spill out.

"Ugh," says Syd.

"Ugh," says Nanci.

Clearly, this side of life, the side where they must reckon with the ebb and flow of dollars and cents, is not their strength. It apparently drains them of vitality. Merely being in the presence of their "financial records" has turned them from the vibrant impassioned artists you know and love, to fretful and lethargic people who offer no more in greeting than "ugh."

You see a gray metal folding chair propped against the wall near the oven. You open it and sit down at the table. The chair is warm, the kitchen is warm. All three of you focus your gaze on the mess of papers spread before you.

Syd slumps deep into his chair. His eyes close. Nanci stares into the scrap pile as though deep in thought, or dazed. You lean forward and rest your cheek against the tabletop. From this vantage, the scraps look like a tiny mountain range of snowy peaks. When you breath, the mountains tremble, like you are a god. Breathe and tremble, breathe and tremble.

You follow this reverie. It leads you into the mountains where you become tiny and the mountains, grand...

"I choose to FIGHT BACK!" cries Syd.

You jerk awake. Syd is standing, his chest heaves and his eyes glow with a defiant fire.

"I can do it!" he shrieks. Then, quietly: "I can organize this mess."

You watch Nanci. She stares up at Syd. In her face you see admiration and pride.

Syd straightens to his full height and addresses you. "Tell me what I must do," he says. "And I shall do it. For whatever it is that must be done, I pledge myself to your service. I will walk the walk. I will make the calls. I will do what is needed."

The spell of lethargy has been broken. You are tempted to burst out in laughter, or ask him where the British accent came from. But you know better.

"First, we pack this mess away," you say, hoping to sound wise and deliberate. "And we make a fresh start."

Syd lunges to the task of repacking the bag. Scraps go into the bag. Scraps go onto the floor. Scraps hit the stovetop and crowd around cold idle burners. Syd presses on until all the scraps are off the table.

You see that you need to move fast. You're not sure how long this valiant energy will last. You issue commands.

"Nanci, you go find all bills that are sent to you each month. I'm talking about bills you receive in the mail, not receipts or notes you take on bits of paper. Just what comes in the mail."

"You mean like for my cellphone and car insurance?" she says.

"Exactly. And Syd, you and I are going to start putting together **income statements** for your business. Then I'll work with Nanci. Finally we'll do one for your personal life, if we still feel like that's needed."

Syd seems to waiver at this instruction. He's probably never used an income statement before, you imagine. Probably makes him nervous because it sounds like some high-finance, bean-counter type of tool.

Income Statement Construction

"The income statement," you say, "is simple. We make a list of your income from all sources, then a list of your expenses. Subtract expenses from income. That's it."

Syd is clearly relieved.

"Well, I made some money from shows over the past couple of years," he says. "How far back you want to go?" "Okay, let's just go with this year. We could even start with just this month, whatever works for you."

You decide to construct his income statement for the time period beginning on December first of this current year. He hosts so few shows, and works on his practice constantly, that it seemed like a fit to do it this way.

He provides you with a blank, coffee-stained sheet of paper. You write "Income" at the top of the page. You slide the sheet toward him and tell him to list the money he made from his brick performance practice.

You remind him to just focus on the bricks. He keeps blurting out income he's gotten from odd jobs, like from the fast food joint he used to work for, the time he cut lawns, or when he helped a carpenter. Before long he gets it: you're only talking about income from his art practice. He lists the various shows he's done, over the past year, and how much he made for each.

During this conversation, Nanci returns with a small stack of paper invoices. She's been listening in. On a clean piece of paper from her sketchbook, she works on an income statement of her own. You lean toward her, but she ignores you. She compiles a list that quickly grows quite long. Things for her are clearly more complex.

After she's made several line items, she moves on to a fresh page. You decide she needs no help from you. Just as you turn back toward Syd, she says "I'm doing mine month by month."

Syd, by now, seems to totally understand the job at hand. He's working on a new list entitled "Expenses." You stand up and watch them scribble and erase. You feel like a grade school teacher who's just handed out a test.

"Can we talk with each other about our answers?" Syd asks.

"Of course, you knucklehead," Nanci replies.

For a moment, it seems they'll begin to fight. But they don't. They pause and face each other again. Their work becomes a discussion.

Sometimes they thumb through the stack of papers Nanci collected. Sometimes one of them asks the other for help remembering a detail.

They hit a moment where they become confused—they don't have any information about out-of-pocket expenses, like groceries, or clothing, or repairs for M-cubed amplifiers.

"Just make the best estimate you can, for now," you say.

"Will that be very accurate?" asks Nanci.

"It won't be perfect. But it will be a good first step. Then we can revisit this in a couple of months to refine it."

You explain that to get an accurate handle on their expenses, they'll have to track what they spend. Starting at the first day of the next month, every day for the whole month, they should write down what they spent that day. Nanci could keep a few pages of her sketchbook for this. If they follow through and really do this, then at the end of the month they should have information they can use to refine the income statements they are creating.

Syd begins to roll his eyes and complain that this all sounds like a lot of work, and he didn't sign up for this, and will there ever be space for simply living his life amidst all this financial bullshit! Nanci looks like she's about to reach over and cuff him. She uses words instead. "Syd. Do you remember that we are in deep doo-doo here? We need to figure this out because we are totally out of control and we both know it. Either we do like the brain says," she nods toward you "or I make you organize the bag. Alone." She nods toward the grocery bag full of receipts.

Syd gets back to work. They continue for another half hour or so. There are no more outbursts, no arguments, just soft murmurs and the sounds of pencil on paper. You go out front to the living room and pick up a guitar you find leaning against a chair. You tune it, then pluck out a song you've been working on. Several minutes pass.

"We're done!" Syd yells.

You stop playing with the guitar and walk back into the kitchen. Nanci is on Syd's lap. Before them on the table are three, neatly written income statements. Each lists income and expenses; each contains artful doodles along the edges. One sheet describes Nanci's band activities, one is for Syd's brick practice, one for their personal lives. They beam at you proudly.

"What do we do now?" Syd asks.

"Well, now," Nanci says as she leans forward over the statements. "Now we take a look at them and try to figure things out."

"Damn, this helps!" she says. "I can use this as my budget. I can totally figure out how to plan for the month ahead. That will be useful."

"Let's eat," says Syd. "I'll gun up the grill."

Cash Flow

"Only thing missing is to figure out how this works with the actual cash balance in my bank account. It's one thing to know what the month might look like. It's another to know whether or not I will have the cash on hand when the time comes to pay for something," Nancy says.

That's cash flow, you tell her. She's talking about cash flow. You take out another piece of paper and show her a rough draft of how she can map out her cash flow on a weekly basis. You don't use a super formal cash flow statement, like the ones used in some publicly traded corporation. You use a simpler approach.

"Write down how much cash is in your account at the beginning of the week. Then write down all the income you expect to come in for the week. Add these numbers up.

"Then below this, write the expenses that need to be paid out during the week. You subtract these from the income plus cash. Whatever is left over, you write at the bottom of the list."

You then show her how she can move this bottom number (the total leftover for the week) up to the top of a new column. This can help plan for the next week.

"At the beginning of the next week, you can check the actual balance in your checking account and see if your estimates are close. If you are off by a bit, you can update your number at the top of the column so you know you're starting from reality."

"I love it," says Nanci.

"Love it?" you ask.

"Yes."

You can tell she means it. She might be a punk rock queen, but she's also a shrewd entrepreneur. Now, she will be back in control of things, they way she usually is. You and she exchange the Michelle/Barack fist bump. Of course it's a foolish thing to do, but it seems somehow fitting.

"I love it too!" crows Syd, who has just come back into the room, a steaming mug in his hand. From the smell, it is clear he has just brewed up a dosage of his special home-remedy tea.

You feel proud of your work, thrilled that it looks like you have helped them. They keep nodding and praising your efforts. Syd begins to openly weep. Nanci leans against him. Then they clink mugs and toast to their success.

Questions to think about:

1. Are formal financial statements like this really necessary for everyone?

2. So they filled out some worksheets, big deal. What comes next?

3. If they decide to use these statements, how might they adjust them to suit their own needs?

4. They both get engaged in the process during the case, but what should they do if one of them loses religion on the process and falls back into old bad habits?

JUST TELL ME HOW

It's a ritual. Anyone doing this kind of planning needs to know that you can't do it just one time. You need to make it a ritual, something you do each year. Then, year by year, you can make great changes in your financial life.

Using Financial Statements

If you were going to organize someone's financial life, there are really only three financial statements that you would use : The Income Statement, The Cash Flow Statement, and The Statement of Net Worth. These three statements are essentially the same whether the entity being analyzed is an individual person or a big company.

Each statement provides a different perspective. Taken together, they tell a well-rounded financial story. Sometimes, one statement might be more important to you than the others. Say you have a cash flow crunch...well, then guess which statement is the one you'd want to construct or refer to? That's right! The Cash Flow Statement! Damn, you're good. Then, if another time, you find you're swimming in debt...the statement you'll want to review is the Statement of Net Worth (okay, so the statement names don't really have to use upper case, like a proper noun. But it does make them look super important, doesn't it?).

The Income Statement - Sometimes called an income and expense worksheet, this shows you how money flows in and out of your life. Income comes in, expenses flow out. The difference between total income and total expenses clarifies whether they are making or losing money.

A corporation or small business would use the same basic format for their own income statement, but their line items would be different, of course. The sample Income Statement on the following page is done on a monthly time frame, but these can be constructed with a different period, like annually or quarterly.

The Cash Flow Statement - This statement helps you figure out where cash is going and whether there is enough to cover expenses during a certain period. If someone is in dire financial straits, they'd want to construct this statement on a week to week, or month to month basis. Skip ahead to the sample Cash Flow Statement.

The Statement of Net Worth - This shows a snapshot in time of someone's financial value. Now, of course someone's value can be judged on a whole lot of different criteria (how are they as an artist, friend, parent, lover, athlete, and so on). This statement only judges the one dimension of money. It's important but not everything. Okay? Skip ahead again to the sample of the Statement of Net Worth.

Income Statement - Not so complex, when you really look at it. Just fill in the blanks. Always slightly underestimate income and slightly overestimate expenses. That way you're more likely to be dealing with reality!

Income	$ per Month	Expenses	$ per Month
		Standard Monthly	
Wages	_____	Savings/Retirement	_____
Tips	_____	Rent/Mortgage	_____
Art Sales	_____	Cell Phone/Internet	_____
Royalties	_____	Electricity	_____
Odd Jobs	_____	Water	_____
Gifts Received	_____	Gas/Oil	_____
Other_____	_____	Cable	_____
Other_____	_____	Car Payment	_____
		Health Insurance	_____
Total Income	_____	Life, Other Insurance	_____
		Loan Payment	_____
		Daycare	_____
		Credit Card Payment	_____
		Other_____	_____
		Subtotal Standard Exp	_____
		Out-of-Pocket	
		Groceries	_____
		Gas/transportation	_____
		Car Maintenance	_____
		Clothing	_____
		Entertainment	_____
		Eating out	_____
		Personal Care	_____
		Charity Donations	_____
		Travel	_____
		Vacation Expenses	_____
		Other_____	_____
		Subtotal Out-of-Pocket Exp	_____
Total Income	_____	**Total Monthly Expenses**	_____

Cash Flow

	Week One	Week Two	Week Three	Week Four
Beginning Cash Balance				

Income

Wages				
Tips				
Art Sales				
Royalties				
Odd Jobs				
Gifts Received				
Other_____				
Total Income				

Standard Monthly

Savings/Retirement				
Rent/Mortgage				
Cell Phone/Internet				
Electricity				
Water				
Gas/Oil				
Cable				
Car Payment				
Health Insurance				
Life, Other Insurance				
All Debt Payments				
Daycare				
Other_____				
Subtotal Standard Exp,				

Out-of-Pocket

Groceries				
Gas/transportation				
Entertainment				
Charity Donations				
Travel				
Other_____				
Subtotal Out-of-Pocket Exp				
Total Monthly Expenses				
Ending Cash Balance				

Using the Cash Flow Statement

In the sample on the preceding page, the statement breaks down cash flow into weekly segments (i.e., each column is a different week). You'd use a weekly cash flow statement for someone who's really living on the financial edge...like Syd and Nanci. If dealing with someone with a bit more leeway, you could do this on a monthly or even quarterly basis. To use this statement, do this:

Beginning Cash Balance - Put your beginning cash balance at the top of column for week one. This is the balance from your available cash, like your checking and savings accounts.

Income - Fill in all of your income for week one. Only include income that you in actuality *receive*. We're dealing with cash here, so only put down income that you get your hands on and either add to your bank account, store in your mason jar, stuff into your pillowcase, etc. If there is any money that you know for certain you are going to receive soon, don't include it here until it is in hand. Got it?

Expenses - Using the same categories as your Monthly Income and Expense Worksheet, fill in the expenses that you pay out in week one. Whether you are paying by check or by cash or debit, mark them down if cash leaves your hands during this week. If you want to be absolutely accurate, you will include a check into your list only once you know it's been cashed.

Net Income/(Loss) - The difference between income and expenses is, as you already know, your net income or loss for the period, in this case week one. See how the word "Loss" is in parentheses? That's the financial industry's way of saying "negative number." If this number is in parentheses, then more cash has gone out than has come in for week one.

Ending Cash Balance - Take the Beginning Cash Balance and add or subtract the Net Income/(Loss) and you have the ending cash balance for week one. This shows whether you have increased or decreased the amount of cash on hand during week one. This should, if you've been careful, match your bank account balance. Of course, it won't exactly, because things never tie out exactly. There'll be some bank fee or credit or some check you forgot you wrote or something that will make the balance change. But you'll be close.

Beginning Cash Balance Week Two - Wait! You're not done! The Ending Cash Balance of week one is the Beginning Cash Balance of week two. Now, with more confidence and swagger, you begin the same process again.

Net Worth Worksheet

While the previous two statements show financial position during a certain period. The **Statement of Net Worth** shows financial position at a snapshot in time: where are we now, today, at this particular moment. For a company, this statement is often called the **Balance Sheet**. For individuals, it is the Statement of Net Worth.

Filling this out requires digging through drawers and folders for old statements and invoices. Fill in all assets, dividing between liquid and illiquid assets (see the glossary for a definition of **liquidity**). Then write down all debts...it can be a real bummer to list all debts right out in the open like this. But fear not, it is better to know. Remember from Chapter One, avoidance can be expensive!

Assets

Liquid

Emergency fund		Held at a bank or Credit Union
Checking account		Where you manage expenses
Individual Retirement Accounts		Traditional IRAs, ROTH IRAs
Retirement Plan Assets		403bs, 401Ks, etc.
Other		Annuities, cash in the mattress, etc.
Other	_____	
Sub total	0	

Illiquid

Residence		Approximate value if sold today
Other Real Estate		"
Tools & Equipment		"
Ownership Share in Business		"
Unsold Inventory		Could you *really* sell your artwork?
Other		Collectibles of value, for example
Other	_____	
Sub total	0	

Total Assets 0

Debt

Mortgage (remaining balance)		Term and interest rate.
Equity Line		Usually a variable rate
Student Loan total		Stafford, PLUS, other
Credit Cards		Aggregate all cards
Personal Debt		Informal or otherwise
Other	_____	
Sub total	0	

Net Worth Estimate _____ Snapshot of a point in time

KEY TERMS

Balance Sheet - This is one of the main statements used if you want to look at something from a financial perspective. If you're looking at a company or not for profit organization, the statement is called a Balance Sheet. If you're looking at an individual person, it's called a Statement of Net Worth. In either case, the statement provides a snapshot of where you or your business stand on a given date.

Cash Flow Statement - This helps you figure out the difference between cash coming in from all sources and cash going out. If the results are negative you have a deficit (like, say, the US government). There is a saying: "cash is king," which can probably mean different things in different settings. But in terms of cash flow, it means that you need to have enough money coming in regularly to pay your bills. If you have a big sum of money coming in soon (from say a grant or a commission), you might be rich when that money arrives, but if you can't pay your bills between now and then, you have a cash flow problem.

Income Statement - This helps you track earnings less expenses for a given period, itemized by category. We also here refer to it as the Income and Expense Worksheet, because developing one of these for yourself or for an organization is an important step in developing a budget.

Liquidity - In finance, the term liquidity is used to describe how quickly an asset can be converted to cash. This is an important concept and you should think of it as a spectrum: highly liquid to illiquid. The most liquid asset is cash (like your checking account or savings). One step down the liquidity scale would be assets like stocks and index funds. At the far end, assets like houses are not very liquid. Also, part ownership in a small private business is a very very illiquid asset.

Statement of Net Worth - Essentially the same thing as the Balance Sheet described above. The Balance Sheet is the term used more commonly for an organization and Net Worth Statement is used for an individual or very small organization.

CHAPTER THREE - PAYING YOUR TAXES

Key Chapter Concepts:
1. Don't avoid your taxes.
2. How to work with a tax preparer.
3. Some tax terms, demystified.

Case Study: It's Not Your Money!

You never earned much from your creative work, not yet. And because the bills kept arriving with relentless regularity, you decided to just bear down and take a part time job—the first decent one you could get. No matter what.

That's how you found yourself one day (horror of horrors!) interning for a local accounting firm. That's right. An accounting firm. You never imagined you'd work in a firm, let alone one that had the word *accounting* in front of it. But they were hiring, and you needed the money.

At the firm, you work as a gofer.

Not an administrative assistant or an apprentice...nope, a gofer.

Or, more accurately, *the* gofer. That's what everyone called you: "Make the gofer go get it," they'ed say, and then they'ed laugh, assuming you were laughing right along with them...

Which, in fact, you were. Because so what? You got to work in a quiet indoor space where your coworkers, the accountants, were in actuality pretty nice people. It never crossed your mind before this, but you found them to be funny, interesting, some of them even...cute.

And it wasn't all just making copies and fetching lunch. There were aspects to the job that you found interesting, though you of course never admit this to your uber-cool art school friends.

For example, none of the firm's bosses (they refer to each other as partners, which makes you want to make life partner jokes...but you decide not to go there) had apparently spent any time ever learning a goddamn thing about technology. So you became the go-to person for all sorts of simple tasks related to computers. Whereas at first you found it annoying to be constantly called in to help someone remember their password, you eventually took on the responsibility as their teacher.

And teaching the partners how to execute basic computer functions eventually became pretty interesting. Once you moved them beyond the basics, like knowing to not panic every time their computer *sleeps*, you started focusing their pointy little heads on more interesting and sophisticated applications, like sending emails and syncing their smart phones with their laptops (they all have both—phone and laptop—and it's almost cute how excited they get when they realize that the two objects can actually work in communication with each other).

But by far, the most interesting part of working with partners comes when you are called in to take notes for meetings with clients. It's not the taking notes part that turns you on so much as hearing clients, who are oddly enough just plain old normal people, talk about issues they face in their daily lives. Hearing how the partners respond to clients made you finally understand why someone would ever want to become something called a Certified Public Accountant (or **CPA)** in the first place.

There was one partner in particular that gained a whole 'nother level of respect from you one day. He's named Rich (which is, if you think about it, a funny name for someone who

works with money). He deals with clients of all types, doesn't seem to care if they are rich or poor, super knowledgeable or clueless. He treats everyone just the same: they're people in need of help. Turns out, he knows many people in the local art scene. He says he has lots of clients who are artists.

"From a tax and business perspective," he says, "artists are often just like small private entrepreneurs. Only many of them don't see themselves that way—or don't want to."

***

One day, you're on your way back from the copier and you notice a guy named Art standing in the firm's reception area, staring at the receptionist. You know Art, have known him for a while, he's a brilliantly talented painter. And from what you know of him, you're flabbergasted to see him here. The receptionist takes one look at Art and calls for Rich.

A moment later, Rich asks you to sit in on a meeting with this potential new client. You're a bit bashful when you step into the conference room, bashful during introductions. Who knows how Art will react to having you on location for the telling of his personal financial story.

Art doesn't seem to recognize you. He shakes your hand (limp handshake, doesn't look you in the eye), sits down, stares at Rich. But, you muse, Art's Art and he can be a bit goofy at times. Maybe seeing you out of context has thrown him for a loop and he just wants to play it cool. Maybe he has forgotten you. You know for a fact that Art has been relatively hard on his short term memory over the years, so maybe your face has just slipped away into the mist of his brilliant creative mind.

Or maybe he's just all stressed out and focused on other matters. After all, something big must be up for him to have ever come in to see an accountant. Who knows what forces conspired to lead him here.

You watch him as he sits. He seems more than uncomfortable. He seems downright rattled. As you sit down and take out a clean sheet of paper, you reflect that it's been a couple of years since you saw him. Last you heard, he was still the prodigious virtuoso, cranking out quality piece after quality piece. After so many years selling all those high priced paintings, he must have quite a bit of money by now.

Rich begins the conversation with small talk, apparently trying to get Art to relax a bit. Art was never one for nice-nice. He launches right in.

"I don't want to go to prison," Art blurts out, to which Rich visibly flinches.

"Uhm, say more," Rich says.

Art leans back in his chair and looks around the room, examining everything, except for Rich. He turns desperate, almost frantic.

Then Art closes his eyes and goes quiet. For a moment. When he opens them again, he's regained control. He draws a breath and begins his story, speaking spasmodically and fast.

You struggle to keep up with your notes. Rich just sits back and listens, occasionally picking up his pen to jot down a thought.

"I don't want to go to prison," Art says again. Only this time, he says it in a calm tone, firm with resolution.

"I've always done well with my painting. It's the only thing I do, only thing I've ever done. My paintings are good, or bad—I don't even know, because it's all I do. I paint."

"You've seen me, right? You know," he gestures toward you, as though just noticing you are in the room.

"And people have always seemed to want my paintings," he continues. "Which used to amuse me. I mean, I thought if someone wants to go through the piles of canvas in my shed and buy stuff, then so be it.

"But I don't see it that way now. Wasn't too long after getting out of art school that I realized I'm not trained to do any other kind of work. I saw that I needed to make a living.

"So I met this woman? At one of my local shows? Her name's Katya and she owns a big swanky gallery in Manhattan. Well, long story short, she got all excited about my work and said she wanted to help me sell my art through her gallery.

"So for the past two years, that's what I've been doing: every couple of months or so, I send a few paintings to her—well actually at first I just threw them in the back of my car and drove them down to her, but when I asked her to help me unload one time in the rain, she got all freaked out and ever since then she insisted that I take them to the UPS store to have them packed and shipped. I keep telling her it's an expensive way to ship, but she says she can afford it, so I let her have her way.

"Anyway, for a while we went on like that. I'd ship the paintings. She'd mail me checks. I'd cash the checks, spend some of the money, put the rest in my stash, and send more paintings. It was all good.

"Then last October, she decided to stop selling my paintings for a little while. She said she wanted to let anticipation build. That people were coming in looking for my work and she wanted to play hard to get or something in order to do a big show in a year or so.

"And she felt bad she had to disrupt my cash flow. I didn't tell her that it didn't matter to me, that I never spent a lot of the money I got from her checks. I'd just leave it in my stash, which is this shoebox I keep under the floor boards in my studio.

"So she gave me a job down at her gallery. I go down there every other week. I do whatever needs to be done, like hanging pictures, sweeping up, or whatever. At night I crash at her brother's place, which is fine because I guess he lives in Europe so I get his loft all to myself.

"I was feeling pretty good about things. I have this super cush job. I get to live in this apartment in the middle of New York. There'll be a big showing of my work some time soon.

"I remember thinking: what could go wrong? Well, basically the same day I asked myself that question, I found trouble. I came back home, to my real home—my studio up here in

Providence, and there was this letter waiting for me from Katya's office. Inside it was this form called a **W-9**?"

Rich nodded, like yes, he's heard of them. Then motions for Art to continue.

"Next time I saw Katya, I asked her what I was supposed to do with that form and she said I should give it to my accountant when I do my taxes this year. She said it's kind of like the **1099s** I "always turn in" (here, Art adds air quotes). I played it cool, like I knew what she was talking about.

"That was three days ago and I haven't slept since. The whole conversation sent me into a panic because I haven't dealt with taxes, basically...ever...as far as I know. I kind of thought I didn't need to deal with that because every gallery I've ever sold through was in charge of paying the taxes so I didn't know I was supposed to pay those taxes too.

"I don't know if I'm in big trouble. I owe at least two years of taxes that I've never paid. I went on the internet and did a ton of searches on tax evasion and now I'm worried that I am going to jail.

Here Art pauses. Takes a breath.

"But I'm prepared to face whatever awaits. I'm not a kid anymore. I want to face my fate like a man. And after my time has been served, I'll start all over again, as an upstanding citizen.

"Who knows? Prison might even improve my work. Heck, might even make it more valuable."

Art goes silent. He seems exhausted but relieved, as if he's confessed to a great burden he's been carrying. Rich leans back in his chair, props his elbows on the armrests and interlocks his fingers.

QUESTIONS AND CONSOLATION FOR ART

"Well, Art," Rich begins. "That's quite a story. But you will not go to jail for this, even if it will improve your artistic career. Generally speaking, the IRS is not out to punish people but to bring them into compliance and have them pay what they owe. You may face penalties if it turns out you owe – *but we do not even know that yet*. Relax.

"Our plan is to reconstruct your finances for the last two years as best we can. It will not be precise but at least we will be able to file, get you back on the right path."

You look on in amazement while Rich's accountant brain kicks into gear. Turns out, once this happens, he speaks in bullet point. Each thought comes out one after the other, allaying Art's fears as the plan is crafted. Rich's comments go something like this:

- Do you have a copy of your last tax return, three years ago?

- What kind of records or numbers can you come up with for your income? Can you or did you get a statement from Katya? You must be able to do that.

- Do you have a separate bank account for your painting income?

- Do you have copies of your bank statements? I know it's a long shot but that might provide some background information about your business activities. (You have a business, you have income, you have income tax.)

- We need to get a sense of how much you made from non-gallery sales. I suspect that will be harder than getting numbers from Katya.

- You are allowed, indeed expected, to take **deductions** for your professional expenses. You only pay taxes on your **net income**. Do the statements from your bank include copies of the checks you wrote? Did you pay anything by credit card?

- Going forward, you will need that separate bank account AND some sort of process to help you track your income and expenses. You could use software or just pencil and paper, so long as you keep track.

- Other expenses – we can deduct your roundtrip business mileage to NYC. How many times did you drive there?

- Can you tell me about what supplies you use? Did you take any courses? Did you pay dues for any memberships? Worst case, again, we estimate: how much paint do you "consume" in an average painting?

- Is your studio part of your residence? We still may be able to take a "home office deduction" if it qualifies. Or was the studio a separate location? Do you have storage fees?

- What percentage of your phone calls and your hours on the phone are for business?

- Do you pay health insurance? That is a deduction.

- How did Katya pay you for your maintenance work? Might you have received a "**W-2**" from her and did you have taxes withheld?

- What is your best projection for this coming year's sales? With artists especially, it is always a crapshoot.

- You should plan to save between 30% and 35% of each art sale for taxes, and we will set you up on a plan for **estimated taxes** for next year.

- You should consider your art business a **sole proprietorship**. That's how we'll have you file—there's no need to incorporate for now.

Rich is done. Art seems happier...much happier. Maybe he understands everything Rich is saying, maybe he understands little. But Art's relief is clear. He didn't commit a major screwup. He won't be going to jail, at least not for this. His sloppiness and neglect can be cleaned up. His negligence might be expensive to him in terms of fees and back taxes. But he'll emerge ready for the years ahead.

You realize you feel relieved too. Maybe, it dawns on you, you should check into taxes your own self.

Why not?

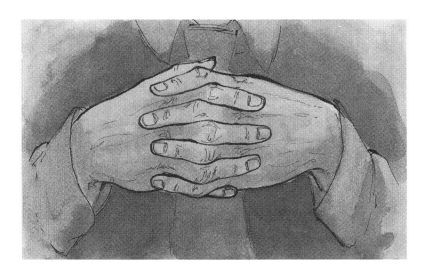

Questions to think about:
1. So, is it realistic to think that the IRS has a process to deal with negligent deadbeats like Art? Isn't Art just opening up a can o' worms by admitting to his negligence?
2. Wouldn't he be better off just ignoring the previous years (what's past is past), and focusing on the present?
3. Isn't there software that a person can use to prepare taxes?
4. If the tax preparation software is so great, why would anyone use a CPA or **tax preparer**?

JUST TELL ME HOW

The topic of taxes is quite a big one, too big perhaps to deal with in just one chapter. We hope this chapter gives you a sense of how to approach paying your taxes and how to seek help.

If You're Behind

Taxes are one of those things you just have to take seriously. Yes, the US system of taxation, spelled out in the dense and labyrinthine Tax Code, is very complex and hard to understand. But, it is your responsibility to do your best to comply. So, do your best.

The IRS, we're sure, knows full well that they are stewards of a process that most Americans have trouble understanding. All you can do as an individual is try to get it right, as in really try to comply (cheezy rhyme...think the IRS ought to use it on their website?). The IRS is likely more interested in getting people to pay their taxes and comply with the code, than trying to catch people and string them up for making mistakes. If you've made a mistake and missed paying something you think you owe, you should find a CPA and tell him/her your story. You would owe any taxes you didn't pay , you might owe

a penalty, and you might be able to work out a payment plan. But usually the process will be pretty straightforward and relatively painless.

Tax Prep Software

Sure, there are many great software applications out there to assist people in preparing and filing. We won't list them here, but a search using some consumer report type of service will help you figure out which one is best for you. These applications keep up-to-date on the different changes to the tax code and have become very intuitive in how they ask you to enter information required.

If you decide to try to file on your own (whether as an individual, home-based business, or whatever) our best advice is to start early. You have until mid April to file (with no **extensions**), so use that time to get things right. If you spend January and the first half of February gathering information and selecting which software you want to use, you could spend the rest of February and all of March entering the data and working through any questions you have. If you run into any trouble spots, the software will have robust help sections that will either let you read handy definitions and instructions, or will connect you with forums and others who can guide you via email or chat.

Finally, tax prep software generally queues you up to be able to file electronically. That is, no paper. This is the way to do it. File online, pay any taxes owed via an electronic draft from your bank account, and any refunds you are due will come back to you faster. Plus, you'll have good records of all of this that you can either print out or save online.

Using a Tax Preparer

Preparing your own taxes might not be for everyone. Some people have situations that are complex, or some people want the confidence of knowing they have a professional to help them get things right. So, paying the fee to hire a CPA or tax preparer is well worth it. One of the key lessons from this case is that a professional tax preparer is in the business of helping people straighten things out so that they can pay their taxes correctly. Because the U.S. Tax Code is complex, CPAs like Rich can help him to make things right. A person like Rich knows which forms need to be filled in with which information. He knows about filing deadlines and extensions and such. This is a job that (we're guessing) Art probably can't do on his own.

Many people rely on a CPA or tax preparer for help. People collect all the information needed (1099s, W-9s, etc.) and dump it on their CPA come late winter/early spring. But, make no mistake about it, filing your taxes is your responsibility, no matter what. A tax preparer can help, but they do not take on your responsibility to pay your taxes. So long as you do your best to file as accurately as can reasonably be expected, you will probably be in good shape.

KEY TERMS AND CONCEPTS

CPA - Also known as an accountant, a CPA is a licensed professional who gets paid to keep you out of debtor's prison. Okay...not really. Or at least not any more. This term refers to a person who's taken and passed a very rigorous course of study to earn the designation "Certified Public Accountant." CPAs can work for big companies, banks, brokerage firms and so on. But most individuals interact with CPAs when they need help preparing and filing their taxes (whether personal or small business/not for profit). A good CPA understands the laws and regulations regarding taxes in the US. They can help you figure out what to do in various tax- and business-related situations. They also are often involved in companies helping to prepare audits and bookkeeping.

Deductions - You pay income taxes on, you guessed it, your income. The US Tax Code offers opportunities for tax filers to reduce the amount of income they have to pay taxes on. Basically, there are many items that the IRS has been asked to put into the Code as exemptions, things that enable a tax filer to reduce their taxable income. So for example if someone made $50,000 per year in income and had $10,000 in deductions, they'd have *taxable income* of $40,000. How are these deductions determined? Well, the best way to understand that is to know that deductions come through the political system (Federal, state, and local). So if politicians want to encourage one sort of behavior in individuals, they can offer a deduction as an incentive. The cynics among us will say that politicians also create deductions as a way to "pay off" their rich corporate campaign contributors...but we'd never be that cynical, right? Since the tax code is a product of the political process, how many guesses you want to make about whether it holds up as a logical, un-contradictory document? Okay, one guess, you get one guess.

Estimated Taxes - If you are a sole proprietor of a business (like an artist, for example!) you do not have taxes withheld from your pay. You still have to pay, but need to manage the tax payments yourself and there are penalties for underpayment. Your estimated taxes are intended to cover your liability from *self-employment tax* as well as state and federal income taxes. You typically pay estimated taxes on a quarterly basis.

Extensions - In the case of tax filing, sometimes a person or company can't get their taxes done and filed by the required date (mid April for individuals). If this happens, the IRS permits you to request an extension, which gives you permission to file a few months later. Use this option if you really have to; it's better to file an extension than to file late, incomplete, or incorrectly. Don't use this if you're just lazy and a procrastinator. In most cases, just get your taxes done and filed on time, and then move on with your life.

Independent Contractor - You get paid for a job and there are no payroll taxes taken out. This makes you a sole proprietor by default, and subject to self-employment tax and estimated taxes.

Net Income - As on the Income Statement or Income and Expense Worksheet, net income is the income that's remaining after all expenses are subtracted. Corporations pay taxes on net income, that is income after cash and non-cash expenses. Individuals pay taxes on taxable income, which is similar: income minus deductions.

Self-Employment Income - Earnings from a sole proprietor's business, net of expenses (which means, what's left over after you take out, or "net out" all expenses).

Sole Proprietor - You are the sole owner of a business that is not incorporated.

Tax Preparer - Come tax season, many people prepare taxes for other people or companies, for a fee. You don't have to have a CPA designation to prepare taxes. Many people work as self-employed tax preparers and use software or their own experience or both to help people get their taxes done. They have a crazy busy season from January through April, and then close down shop and go back to their other lives as artists or fishermen or vagrants or whatever.

W-2 - The tax form employees receive annually, showing earnings and withholdings. Brought to accountant or hidden in drawer.

1099 - Statement of annual earnings for a sole proprietor, copy goes to the IRS.

CHAPTER FOUR - THE GRANT RANT

> **Key Chapter Concepts:**
> 1. How to prepare a grant application.
> 2. Setting expectations.
> 3. What *not* to do.

Case Study: Gimme the Money

Your job with Rich the accountant was great, but once tax season ended it got kind of quiet around the firm. Too quiet. So you took the financially ill-advised step of quitting a paying job and taking an unpaid internship.

The internship is a good one. It's at the Arts Council, a local foundation that gives grants to artists! You tried to get a grant from "the Council" a year or so back. Got shot down. So landing this (unpaid) internship felt like retribution of sorts, like maybe they thought you were great all along, even though they rejected your application, and now they are bringing you into their inner sanctum because you're so special and unique. You go to work energized your first day. You have big plans.

In the first hour of your first day, you sit with Claire, the receptionist and knower of all things Council. You meet with her in the Council's main conference room, a room with comfortable chairs, a large table, and fascinating posters on the walls about projects they've funded in the past. She explains the

menial data entry work you'll be doing—you know it is menial because that's the word she uses to describe it—but she also explains how important it will be to have all the prior years' grant info accessible electronically. So by the time she finishes explaining things to you, you feel important, very important indeed. Yours is perhaps the most important job in the entire Council.

Enthused and emboldened by your own awesomeness, you tell Claire about your grant application they rejected a year ago. You wonder aloud whether their rejection had anything to do with their bringing you on as an intern—maybe, you say, you made such a good first impression that they rejected you so that they could hire you later.

She fixes you with an odd stare and says no, that wasn't it. You want her to say more, but just then the door to the conference room opens and loveliness herself walks through the room.

Charity Grantham is her name. Claire introduces you, and Charity says hello and offers you a smile that passes right through your eyes and continues on into you, where it simultaneously warms and chills your very guts. You respond to her hello with a sort of gasping retch, and struggle to affect some sort of expression on your face that conveys anything in the realm of normal and pleasant.

She laughs as though delighted by your predicament, then welcomes you aboard, then turns to leave the room. She saved you and you are now hers. Her eyes are dark. Her hair is darker —she wears it in a style that is at once both contemporary and traditional. Her style of clothing is much the same: a kind of cross between Jazz Age flapper, Manhattan advertising account executive, and librarian.

Everything about her says money. And taste. But also accessibility and poise. You are enthralled.

Your trance is finally broken when Claire shakes your shoulder.

"That's Charity," says Claire. "Charity Grantham. She's the grants director here. All Council money passes through her hands. Charity is, quite simply, the best."

The best, you think to your self. You can say that again. She is the best! You hope you're not talking out loud. But of course, your thoughts are most likely plain for Claire to read. You've met philanthropic perfection, and her name is Charity.

When you finally come around again, you see that you are now alone in the room. A Post-it note, from Claire, is stuck to the table before you. It says that you've covered enough ground today; come back tomorrow to dig in. You never saw her place it there. How could you have missed it?

You unstick the note. Crumple it and toss it, basketball-style, toward the trash can. You miss. No matter. You can pick it up when you leave. You'll leave in just a moment. After you think a bit more about Charity.

***

Over the next several days, you settle in to your work at the Council. You enter data. Much data. And mindless as the work is, you find that you are beginning to learn about the process of making grants. No, you don't learn this from the data entry so much as from listening and observing what goes on in the office around you.

You'd like to say you learned so much because of your keen observation skills. But that would only be true in part. You do have keen observation skills, of Charity. By watching her, you learn all.

It's a relatively quiet and hardworking office, after all. People work with their doors open, so they can have ready access to each other. When Charity talks to her colleagues, on the phone, or to walk-ins, you pay attention to what's said. Plus, the fact that you selected the desk closest to her office door didn't hurt the acoustical integrity of your eavesdropping.

As you watch, you learn (with no small amount of jealousy) that Charity is popular. Everyone in the office goes to Charity for advice. All the artists you've ever known or even heard of, seem to have at one point or another either called her or turned in an application.

So you're not exactly surprised when different friends of yours turn up at the Council offices, seeking grant funding.

They each arrive and present themselves to Claire the receptionist with the same expectant energy. They each sound (to your ears) like awed adolescents when they ask to speak with *Charity Grantham*. They each ignore you completely. Or fail to notice you. But you think ignore. Which only makes you listen in all the harder.

Syd came in first.

He seemed like such a child as he asked for and then was led to Charity's office. Charity graciously welcomed him and asked him to sit, make himself comfortable. You heard a chair creak as Syd sat onto it. Then you heard him snuffle and let out a small belch. Seems, you grin to yourself, Syd took her seriously when she suggested he get comfortable. Then there was a moment of silence during which you assume Charity is either in shock because of the spectacle of Syd, or she is reading something.

The silence doesn't last long, because Syd—never one to contain his thoughts—begins to talk.

"I am a puppeteer. My puppets are my family, my children," Syd says. "I present intimate shows to an audience of one. The intimacy is critical to the stories I want to tell.

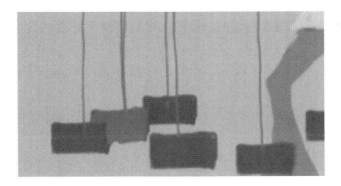

"I have been doing this for quite some time now—ever since I left the cooperative with my college friends. Which was quite an experience, while it lasted. It's where I met the love of my life, Nanci (or where we became a, you know, a couple).

"The co-op was also where I first became introduced to my puppets. I work, you see, in brick. My puppets are brick, native, naked brick. I came across a pile of them just laying against and atop one another. They were just there, alone in an abandoned room.

"I sat with them for hours that day, and for days thereafter. I felt like I'd met my kin. I untangled them, one from another, and arranged them, cleaned them, and held them. Through that process, I came to know them. They released their essence unto me.

"So when I left the co-op and went on the road with Nanci, I released my bricks from that room. I brought them with me, some hundred and fifty (one-fifty-three to be exact). They have been with me ever since.

"Which is why I am here today. Traveling with my family of brick has put quite a strain on my main and only mode of transportation, the Westfalia. The additional and constant weight of the bricks has caused much wear and tear on Westy. It's gotten to where I cannot even use her to travel to shows. She just sits in the driveway alongside the house.

"I need her in order that my practice can grow. I've received some serious interest from potential audiences in far reaches of this state, and beyond. I need to buy new struts, brakes, and a clutch. That's why I've come to you today, Miz Chastity. I have come to ask you to help me get Westy back up and running, so that she can carry me and my brick family. You all are widely admired for the assistance you provide to artists in this state. This is the assistance I need."

As Syd finished his soliloquy, you heard something thump upon Charity's desk. You could only hope that it was not his fist lowered to the desk in emphasis, but you knew Syd well enough to suspect that that was the case.

After a moment of silence—a very brief moment—you heard Charity's terse response.

"Well, Syd, that is quite a story. Clearly you are very passionate about your work. I must say your work sounds interesting indeed. But, I'm sorry to say that we do not fund this type of project."

You could almost hear Syd slump at this news.

"I don't want you to see this as in any way a negative judgement on the value or quality of your creative practice," Charity continued. "In fact, I urge you to review our grant guidelines and see if one of our existing programs might be a match for you in some other area of your work. You can review our guidelines either on our website, or I can get you a brochure on your way out."

With that, the meeting was complete. You beamed at them as they passed by on their way to the front desk; neither of them returned your gaze. Syd shuffled along, looking diminished, like he'd just been rejected by the homecoming queen. As for Charity, she strode past, lovely as ever. You marveled at her kindness toward Syd as she assisted him slowly to the door. It was clear that she'd delivered many a rejection in her day, and she did it with firmness but certainty. It made you love her all the more.

***

The next day, Art arrived at the Council front desk and presented himself to Claire, mumbling that he had an appointment with Charity.

"Oh yes," said Claire. "She's expecting you."

Of course she's expecting *him*, you thought as he passed by. He's the great white hope. The prodigy. The artist that everyone just loves and wants to be seen with.

And you know just why he's here too. He's raising money for a massive outdoor mural across from City Hall. You know this because he told you about it last night while you and he

consumed many plastic cups of beer at the Dean's list function last night back on campus (of course neither of you were ever on the Dean's list, and weren't even students anymore...but no one seemed to care; the school had provided the beer and you two still blended in).

It surprised you that Art never mentioned this meeting last night. But then, maybe you hadn't told him about your internship here. Maybe you were too busy reminiscing. Maybe you didn't want him to meet Charity. Who knows?

As he passes by, your eyes do not meet. You see he has on the same shirt as last night, a stretched and torn black Sex Pistols tee shirt, the same one he always wears. With his elbow, he pins a disorganized stack of paperwork against his ribcage.

"Arthur!" Charity exclaims as he enters her office. "So nice to see you again!"

Again, she says? See you again? You make enough of a groan that Claire leans forward and locks eyes on you with a stare no one could mistake.

"I'm very pleased that you have finally come in to see us," Charity continued. "I must say, I've followed your work for years and I'm looking forward to finding the way to work with you."

"Uhm, thanks," says Art.

You hear chairs scrape floor as they sit. You hear papers drop to the floor and then oopses and here-you-goes as they are recollected. Then you hear Art speak. From the moment he begins, you can tell that he sounds, shall we say, inappropriately prepared for this meeting. You lean back with glee. Art, you know, is both a tremendously talented painter and a tremendous explorer of mind-altering substances. If he wakes up nervous, which would include most days, he in one way or another imbibes. Today was, apparently, no different.

You permit yourself to indulge in a wicked grin.

"Uhm, I know you've seen my paintings, right? And, when we talked on the phone I told you about my mural project? I have the permit and everything, but what I don't have is some of the materials and supplies? This is going to take a lot more stuff than I usually work with so it's kind of expensive."

So far, so good. Charity sits silent, listening. You wait, because you know Art.

"I was thinking that the Council could help me? I saw on your website that you fund large installation type projects like this? I printed out the application from your website. I'm not very good at writing things like this, so when you said come in I figured I'd just bring it with me and we could, like, fill these out together? So that way I'd make sure that I did everything the right way so you can give me the money?"

There is silence in the room. For quite some time. Long enough that you hear Art begin to shift about in his chair.

"Uhm, no," says Charity finally. "I'm afraid that's not quite how it works. I can't fill this out with you or for you. It's the responsibility of applicants to fill out their own applications."

You can tell she wants to add "duh!" at the end of that last sentence. But she restrains herself. When she speaks, you hear the tension in her voice.

"Arthur, your artwork of course has a great following. There is certainly interest here at the Council to work with artists of your talent and potential. But you are clearly not ready for this grant cycle. My advice is that you go back to the drawing board with this, and prepare a complete application for our next grant cycle in six months."

With that, the meeting is concluded. They pause in front of your desk, Art looks confused and Charity looks a bit, well, miffed. She gestures with a sweep of her hand at the front desk and Art ambles towards it. He doesn't say thank you or goodbye, to Charity, you, Claire, or anyone. He says nothing at all. But he seems intrigued by artwork hanging on the walls just beside the front entrance.

Then he leaves. Empty handed.

Claire stares beyond you to Charity, shrugs, and goes back to her work. Charity turns and goes back to her desk. The wheels of her chair whine softly as she sits down. You hear her sigh. Then hear the sound of key strokes as she types—with startling rapidity.

***

An hour or so later, Nanci arrives in front of Claire and asks to speak with Charity. Claire asks Nanci to wait while she sees if Charity is still on the phone. Charity apparently heard that, because she is already out of her office and striding down the hallway past you.

"Hello, Nanci! Thank you for coming in," she says.

They shake hands and then Nanci follows Charity back to her office. As they pass you, Nanci meets your eye. She seems to register you with some surprise, but she doesn't say anything.

She's dressed up, to some extent. She has on her best leather jacket, and crisp black jeans, and frilly kind of blouse. Under her arm she carries a leather bound folio. You almost guffaw: Nanci with a folio? This is the woman who carries her bass guitar in a tattered gig-bag that still has traces of dried blood on it from the notorious Canton, Ohio tour back in 2009.

As she passes you by and turns to step into Charity's office, you have a view of her full ensemble. She looks fabulous, striking, and *ready*.

They get right to business. You hear Nanci present her application.

"I really appreciated your response," Nanci says. "I thought about your comments and could really see how they make my overall proposal more solid. So, thank you."

"Well, they were of course just suggestions," says Charity. "The first draft that you showed me had pretty much everything in it already. It was just a matter of clarifying your points a bit. So I was happy to help."

Then they fall into a long discussion about details of the proposal. Their tones drop to businesslike murmurs. They are clearly reviewing copies of the application and without a copy in front of you, you find their conversation hard to follow. Nanci, it seems, is planning a concert and lecture series that presents her music as a derivative of Gregorian chant. Now *that*, you realize, is something you'd like to see.

Charity and Nanci talk on for at least twenty more minutes. As far as you can tell, they discuss the structure of the program, something about a publicity plan, and of course the budget.

"Okay, it all seems to be here," Charity says. "Are you ready to submit this, or do you want to work on it some more?"

"Well, I guess I want to go over it one more time," Nanci says. "And then I'll submit. Your deadline is at the end of the month, right, so I'm fine if I submit next week?"

"Yes, that's right," says Charity.

"I understand you're doing all online submissions this year. I spent some time on your site and I think I should be totally comfortable with that process."

"Great," says Charity. "We'll look forward to receiving the application. Our grant review committee meets next month to review all applications. So you should know their response a week or so after that. But at this stage I can say that I think you are submitting a very strong application."

"Well, thanks for all your help! I'll keep my fingers crossed."

"You've really done your homework here, Nanci. I don't think you'll need luck. But I wish you good luck all the same!"

Questions to Think About:
1. What did Syd do wrong on his application?
2. What did Art do wrong?
3. What did Nanci do right?
4. Does this mean her approval is assured?
5. Does Charity have the authority to approve an application? Does she have the authority to reject?
6. How would you go about getting a grant?

JUST TELL ME HOW

In this case, Nanci did everything right whereas Syd and Art did everything wrong. For the most part, **grant making organizations** aren't unknowable black boxes or popularity contests or high court judges of worthy work. They are generally places that give money in the form of **grants** to support certain types of work.

How can you know what type of work they support? They tell you. That's right, they explain, through their **submission guidelines**, exactly what they will and will not fund. And how. If you are interested in receiving a grant from a certain organization, and you have not read and understood their submission guidelines, then don't submit an application. Read their guidelines. Learn what they want to fund and how they want you to approach them.

Sometimes, artists look upon grant making organizations with a sense of shyness bordering on intimidation: you need the money, they have the money, and therefore you fear them.

It doesn't have to be this way. In fact, it shouldn't. In the world of arts (and music and culture and humanities), most grant making organizations are staffed by super cool and committed people (many of whom are creative practitioners themselves). They work hard to find cool stuff like yours to support. They may provide support such as grants (that is, money), and they may provide other forms of support as well (such as education, or training resources, or exposure, or connections).

They work within certain published criteria or guidelines. They can't just give out money to whomever they want. So if you have an amazing public installation sculpture project, they might see it as amazing too. But if they only give grants to poets or opera singers, then they'll never give money to your sculpture project. Ever. Unless they change their guidelines. Which they won't do. At least not during this **grant cycle**. You need to understand what their submission guidelines are and then see whether your work is a fit for their guidelines.

Okay? Good...we've probably waaaay overemphasized this point. But that is usually the biggest complaint of grant makers: applicants don't understand the guidelines.

Above, we mentioned grant cycles. That's another important thing to know. Some grants, usually smaller ones, are given out on a **rolling grant** basis. Larger grants are usually administered on a once a year or twice a year cycle. That means that there can be one or two deadlines each year (say April and October) when grant applications are due. Then after applications are received and reviewed, there will be another date when acceptance/rejections notices are sent out.

Grants officers stick to these deadlines. They have to. If you have the greatest application that has ever been submitted, ever, but you missed the deadline...well, tough cookies. You have to work within their time frames.

Now, if this seems like you have to know a lot about an organization, before you ever even submit a grant application, then you are reading this correctly. You should learn about the organization first. Get to know as much as you can about them. You'll know if they seem like a good fit for your work. If they aren't a good fit, then don't bother. Don't try to shoehorn your work into their guidelines. That is usually a bad idea that can lead, at the very least, to wasted time and energy.

You can learn about the organization you are targeting in many ways. Go online and research their submission guidelines. Or call them and request literature. You might also be able to find people who have already received grants from the organization; maybe you could contact them. So long as you're polite, prepared, and respectful of their time, many people will be willing to talk with you.

Also, the grant making staff are often available to speak with potential **grantees**. Different places have different policies on this. But there are a good many grant making staff (called things like the grants director or grants officer) who make it a point to make themselves available to potential applicants. Of course, if you have the chance to talk with a grants officer, or even meet with one in person, you must first be sure you are prepared. Don't go in to that meeting cold. You'll be wasting their time and yours. Plus, you are presenting yourself when you interact like this. So take care to make a good impression. If you are prepared, knowledgeable, and organized, you'll come across that way. You can still ask questions, even dumb ones. Just don't ask questions that could have been answered if you had spent two minutes on their website.

KEY TERMS

Grant - Money given to an applicant to be used as specified in the application. So, if you get a grant to, say, build a super cool installation outside a library, don't use that grant money to go visit friends in Ohio! Use the money as intended: a well meaning gift that is intended to support your work.

Grant Cycle - Grant making organizations often operate on an annual cycle. They accept submissions up to a certain date; review them for a period of time; and they make decisions and notify applicants after a certain date. Then, the next year, they do it all again. Note that they may have just one major application deadline each year; or they may have several different deadlines. But then, of course you'll have this all figured out because you'll read their submission guidelines.

Grant Making Organizations - These are, as the name implies, organizations that give out grant money. They might be private foundations (where some rich person sets up a fund to be used to make grants toward particular needs). Or they might be parts of big corporations (often called something like the charitable giving department). Or government agencies (like a local arts or humanities council). They usually focus their giving on specific areas: arts, poverty, education, and so on. You know...things that no one makes money doing, but they do them anyway because the work is worthy and needs to be done.

Grantees - These are the people seeking grants. Also called applicants, or starving artists.

Grants Officer - This is the person within a grant making organization that administers the grants process. They publicize their organization's grant process and cycle, work with applicants during and after the grant process is complete, and they notify applicants of whether their application got accepted or rejected. They also may provide field support, such as setting up workshops or helping grantees comply with grant guidelines. They are usually great people to know and work with! But don't expect that they are the ones that make the yes/no decisions. Most organizations consider grant applications through a committee process.

Submission Guidelines - These are the "how to" instructions that grant making organizations publicize so that potential applicants can know whether to submit an application and how.

They are usually very carefully worded and provide everything you could reasonably want to know about whether you should pursue a grant from a certain organization. They are a vital source of information. Many applicants ignore them. Or only give them a quick read...which results in? That's right, rejection. Read the submission guidelines, first.

Rolling Grants Cycle - Sometimes, grant applications (especially for smallish grants) are accepted, reviewed, and approved throughout the year, without a specific deadline in place. This means, if you were applying for a grant with a rolling application cycle, you could apply any time during the year. Even still, it would probably make sense to understand if there is a better or worse time throughout the year to try to tap into this process. For example, you might not want to submit right before the holidays or right before their other major grant deadlines.

CHAPTER FIVE - DEBT

Key Chapter Lessons:
1. How to manage debt.
2. A livable debt reduction plan.
3. Details of how credit scores work.

Case Study: Yeehah! Free Money!

Prudence is annoyed. More than annoyed, she is angry. She says she feels disillusioned, used, lied to, scammed. And she's not talking about her last romance—no sane person would dare treat her this way.

It's not personal, at least not for her oppressor. Maybe that's what is making Prudence so mad. Her oppressor barely knows her, on the phone acts like everything is Prudence's fault, misspells her name, wouldn't know her if they met on the street. While for Prudence, it's personal. Intensely personal.

Prudence called you. Said she needed to vent. Meet her tomorrow. At the Roastal Coaster. 10AM. Then she hung up.

That's all she said. You were more than surprised. You never get off the phone with Prudence in less that thirty minutes (of listening). Something had to be up. Something big. You love Prudence, in spite and because of all her Prudence-ness. She'd been your roommate in college, you helped her establish an

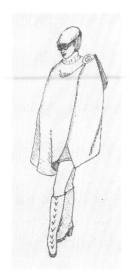

artist co-op with a group of friends, you've collaborated with her on countless projects. You want to help.

Normally, she's the one who has everything buttoned down into a perfect plan. Sounds like her ability to manage every detail of a project has finally come up short. Perhaps this time, you can help her figure things out.

You hurry to the Roastal Coaster (which used to be the Coastal Roaster until it was sold a few years back to a hippy couple with a dyslexic sense of humor). You get there a few minutes early to order your beverage of choice (cafe americano with maple syrup...it's good, try it!), and to stake out a space at one of the good tables over by the windows.

Prudence shows up at, of course, exactly 10:00. She's dressed all in black, as always, with tight leggings stretched over her narrow legs, a loose, wool turtleneck sweater, and a cape clasped at the shoulder with a silver broach that you look forward to inspecting when she is near.

She responds to your wave with the briefest of nods as she places her order. You know what she's getting: jasmine green tea, always the same for her. Then she makes her way over to your table, focusing her intense dark eyes on her ceramic mug, taking care that she doesn't spill a drop.

She places her mug onto the table, sits, and, as she crosses her legs at the knee, takes a moment to direct your eyes down toward the boots she wears: they are of suede, with a great deal of laces and sturdy platforms that add an imperceptible inch or two to her diminutive self. You smile in approval. She swings her knees deftly under the table and the boots are no longer visible to you. She does not return your smile because she needs no affirmation; she knows she looks great.

"Prudie? What's up?" you venture. Few are they who call her Prudie. Even fewer are those who call her Purdie, as in Purdie Prudie, a show of affection you rarely venture to employ.

"Oh, it's such a disaster, a complete f*&%ng mess. I had it all worked out, completely planned so that I could manage my admittedly tight finances and even leave room to build up a little bit of a cushion.

"But now that's all completely blown up. *Universally* blown up, I should say," and laughs bitterly.

"So now I can't make any of it work and I just don't know what to do because my cash flow has gone negative and I have to dip into savings. Only my savings aren't enough to cover my debts because the smaller ones are the expensive ones and the larger ones have lower rates and therefore are the ones I should take care of first but my savings would only be a drop in the bucket. And I set this all up in the first place so that I could finish my studio and be able to work in the daytime, when I'm still sharp.

"Only now, it looks like I'll have to take on more hours at the library and they only have daytime hours which means *so long* to approaching my creative work with a fresh mind. Looks like I'll have to go back to working in the middle of the night which leaves me exhausted all the time and causes me to do crappy artwork

and generally behave like a cranky wench to everyone I come across, which I have to admit right now I don't even care about because I can't deal with anything because I'm so upset about my finances."

With that, she goes silent. You regard your friend as she gazes into her jasmine green tea. She takes a sip, her first. As you watch her, you notice how the strain shows on her face. Her lips seem taut, the smudge of fatigue shows underneath her eyes.

"Prudie, what are you talking about?" you ask, gently as you can; for you have no idea what she is talking about, no idea whatsoever. Something to do with money and not enough of it. But as to the particulars, she's just not making any sense.

But you know how to manage Prudence, when she gets so worked up about something. You take your time, change the subject so that she can take an emotional breather. You focus on her boots: tell her you just love them and ask where she found them. Prudence never pays retail, and prides herself on her talent for finding amazing items in unusual places.

Bingo. The boots bring her back from the brink. For a time she's the normal Prudence again, the one who scours yard sales, thrift stores, eBay and Craig's List, finding beautiful clothing and accessories at even more beautiful prices. No one but no one can do this and make it look as chic as Prudence.

After she walks you through the provenance of each article she's wearing, even those that aren't readily visible, you coax the conversation back to the issue at hand. By now you have each added a currant scone to your repast and have settled in.

Bit by bit, in pieces and clumps, you begin to understand Prudence's dilemma. It's a story you've been through with her before: a classic case of what happens when perfection collides with reality.

It goes like this.

Prudence is excellent with budgeting. Her meticulous approach to all things makes her deft at managing the relation between her expenses and incomes. For years, she's had her budget in balance. Though she didn't make much income, first as a student and then in the years after graduation, she found ways to keep enough ahead of her bills that it all worked. She'd sell some of her artwork (meticulous line drawings, almost like an architect's drafting, of birds, fish, flowers), and supplement her art income with a part time job at the university library, where her skills in cataloging are in hot demand.

As for expenses, she always keeps them in check. She owns a condo that doubles as both her home and studio workspace. It's in an emerging part of the old city, so will one day likely prove to have been an excellent investment. She artfully uses and reuses everything: supplies, fabrics, food. She has figured out how to live well on very little.

So it came as a surprise when she spoke of financial trouble. Of all your mutual art friends, she was the last one you'd ever think would get in a bind over money.

Her problems began when she decided to renovate her studio. She discovered she had to replace the windows. They were old and leaky, causing her space to be too cold in the winter and too damp in the summer. The cold she could handle, but the dampness wrought havoc with storage of her supplies and artwork.

To pay for renovations, almost fifty-thousand dollars, she had to get creative. She didn't qualify for an equity loan to cover the entire amount. The person she spoke with at the local credit union said that, because of her mortgage and outstanding student loan balance, her income would only support an equity loan of twenty-five thousand.

To get the rest, she got clever. She researched, and found, cheap money. Online she found a credit card that charged only

1% **interest** for the first year. She discovered a 2% interest rate card from a poster in the lobby of a bank. And, in what she thought of as a stroke of brilliance, from one of the big box home improvement stores, she got a loyalty card that charged

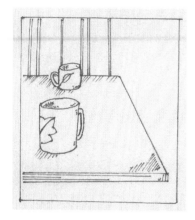

no interest whatsoever if she made all payments on time and within twelve months.

By combining the equity line with the purchasing power of these three cards, she was able to come up with the fifty-thousand. Of course she figured out the monthly payments she'd have once she borrowed all of this. Because the rates were so low, she determined she could cover the payments, with money to spare.

She borrowed:

$25,000 as an equity loan

$20,000 on the two low interest credit cards

$5,000 on materials with the home improvement charge card

If You Want to Make God Laugh...

She borrowed the money, made the renovations, and began to enjoy the great benefit of the improved workspace. As for repayments, the plan worked. It was tight but it worked. At least it did for several months.

Then something happened that she hadn't accounted for. One of the galleries that sold her work went out of business.

"The owner left town and I haven't seen or heard from him since," Prudence said with hushed incredulity.

"He owed me, still owes me, about two thousand dollars. But he just plain didn't pay. He changed his phone number, moved to God knows where, and now I can't find him or talk with him. It's unbelievable."

Unbelievable maybe, but true nonetheless. The gallery owner's transgression couldn't have come at a worse time. She was counting on that two thousand from him. And when it didn't come in, she was short on cash flow and had to decide to pay a couple of her bills late.

She hated to do it but she had no choice. She decided to be late on the card with the lowest interest rate: the home improvement store card. When her paycheck came in from the library a week later, she made the late payment, plus the penalty, immediately.

She figured that was that. She'd do whatever she could to make sure it didn't happen again. When her next bill came for the home improvement card, she opened it and read it carefully. She saw that they charged her a late fee, which hurt but was what she had expected.

"I'd read up on credit cards, you see," Prudence said. "I knew that they can't hit me with **universal default** anymore because that was banned according to the **Credit CARD Act of 2009**. But of course those f*%$ers always find a way to get you!"

A few days later, she received a letter from one of her credit card companies. Assuming it was a solicitation of some sort, she almost tossed it onto her desk without reading it. Thank goodness she changed her mind and opened it. In the envelope was a nasty letter from the credit card company, the one she'd gotten from the bank, saying that they were considering canceling her account.

She was appalled. She'd always paid that card on time and more than the minimum amount. She called them immediately.

"Turns out, after I finally was able to speak with an actual person, that there is still some recourse card companies can use if you mess up on any of your cards, regardless of who issued the card. I guess it was never banned as part of the CARD Act.

"I got so mad that I threatened to close the card and move my business elsewhere. The woman in the call center, sounding all smug and la dee dah just said that she wouldn't do that if she were me because closing a credit card can hurt my **credit score**. And that even if I try to move to another card, I won't qualify for a lower rate card because any new issuer will know that I am a risk for default."

So now Prudence walks around in fear that if she hits any other problems, then her cards will be cancelled, she'll ruin her credit score, and it will take years to dig out.

She pays the minimum balance on each card, every month, and puts any money left over into a savings account, so that she'll have a cushion if she ever has another shortfall. She turns and fixes you with her dark eyes. You see frustration in her eyes. In fact, you see fear.

"What should I do?" she asks. "How in the world will I get out of this mess?"

> **Questions to Think About:**
> 1. What flaw(s) can you see in Prudence's plan?
> 2. Do you agree with her solution?
> 3. What do you think about her reaction?
> 4. How well did she handle the call to the credit card issuer?
> 5. What might she have done differently?
> 6. What should she do now?

JUST TELL ME HOW

Prudence has done many things right in the way she manages her financial life. But she also has done some things wrong. As organized and diligent as she is, she still has a lot to learn. Her case brings to mind three areas to talk about in detail: one, she's been too clever for her own good; two, her debt repayment plan; and three, the way credit scores really work.

Too Clever by Half

Prudence set up a plan that was meticulous and airtight...but it didn't work. Her plan was kind of like the ancient Mayans, who developed an intricate and sophisticated understanding of their known world. Problem was, they didn't understand what was outside of their known world, such as Spaniards.

While it was the business failure of the gallery that finally tripped her up, we don't think that was her main challenge. Nor was her main challenge the maddening minutia of the credit card regulations.

As she crafted her financial plan, Prudence didn't take into account the inescapable fact that life happens. She did not build in room for flexibility. Even the most comprehensive and exacting of plans can end in failure if they don't leave room for the unknown. Unforeseen factors will always come up and you'll have to deal with them.

So how to plan for the unknowns? The simple answer is to expect them. Prepare for them. In financial plans, one way to express this preparation is as an emergency fund (or rainy day fund, or contingency fund, or buffer, or whatever you want to call it).

There are many rules of thumb people use to figure out how much you should have in your emergency fund: enough to cover 3 months of expenses, enough to cover 6 months, nine months, a year. The exact amount depends on how much you can afford (obviously) and how secure you want to feel.

For starters, try to just start with something. Put away a bit each month, say $50 or $100. More if you can afford it. Something is much better than nothing. If you can only get that emergency account up to a thousand dollars, that's great. It'll be helpful in a crisis. Keep building on it. The more you have, the safer you are.

Set good clear plans in place, but don't expect the world to conform to them. As goes the old saw: expect the best, but prepare for the worst.

Debt Repayment Plan

Unless you come into a big chunk of money (inheritance, lottery, mana from heaven), there is no easy way to get out of debt. Debt works that way: it's really easy to get into debt, and hard as heck to pay your way back out.

So if you have a situation like Prudence's, where you have many different debts, spread about on various accounts and cards, here's a good way to pay it off. This approach takes time (as in years), but if you're diligent, it will work.

1. First, get current on all of your payments and stay current.
2. Pay the minimum balance on all of your debts, except for the smallest debt (lowest principal balance).
3. For the smallest one, pay as much more per month as you can reasonably afford.
4. Make sure that extra amount is applied to principal (not to future payments).
5. Keep focusing your extra payment energy on that smallest debt each month until that one is paid off (bravo, now you have one less monthly bill!).
6. Then, take that extra cash flow and focus in the same way on the next smallest debt.
7. Keep that up until it is paid off (now you'll have more cash flow, again).
8. Focus on the next smallest, and then the next. And so on.

Again, this is not a fast process but it works. This means you won't be focusing on paying down the one with the highest interest or the largest outstanding balance. The point is to try to focus on cash flow. You want to pay down debts that you can get rid of quickly, freeing up cash flow that you can use.

If fate smiles upon you and you do come into some money, be sure to do two things with it: save some and use some to pay down debt. As with the process above, pay down the smallest debts first. You want to make a meaningful difference in your monthly expenses.

Credit Scores

Many people find the topic of credit scores intimidating. Think about it. There is a grand infrastructure in place designed to track your every financial transaction and then pass judgement about you. It's like the old joke: you're not paranoid if they really are out to get you.

But, that's the world we live in. Lenders, vendors, and other businesses do indeed have a legitimate need to understand who they are doing business with. When big companies spend vast amounts of time and treasure to compile information about you, you should really try to understand something about what they gather and why. Don't you agree?

So how do credit scores work?

For starters, the most widely used credit score (or FICO Score, see more on this in Chapter One) is actually a combination of scores developed by three different companies: **Transunion, Equifax,** and **Experion.** These three companies, called **credit bureaus,** each have their own networks for gathering information, and their own processes for turning your information into a rating or score. An excellent score is over eight hundred; a score in the low five hundreds isn't so good; below that shows you're in real financial trouble.

These scores focus on several categories in your personal financial life. In rough order of importance, they are:

1. Your payment history: do you pay everything on time? Are you delinquent with anything? If you're delinquent on even the smallest little department store card, you hurt your overall score.

2. How much do you owe in total? Obviously, having a huge amount of outstanding debt can be seen as a problem.

3. Evidence of financial hardship. If you have any tax liens on property or if you have sought credit counseling (see section below on credit counseling), your score will be negatively affected.

4. The length of your track record. A brief track record might mean you have less experience with money. This may or may not be true, but credit bureaus only react to data they can gather.

5. The type of debt you have. If you have a preponderance of revolving credit, such as credit cards, then your score would be lower.

6. Amount of new debt. If you are frequently opening new accounts, it could be a red flag for lenders. Be very careful and deliberate about what new accounts you apply for. Don't overdo it.

Checking Your Score

By law, you are allowed one free credit report every twelve months. You should periodically check your score, so that you have a sense of where you sit in the eyes of this omnipotent and flawed bureaucracy. Periodically reviewing your credit information will alert you to any errors or problems with their data. If you find something in your score that you know is incorrect, you should contact the credit bureau immediately and ask about their process for correcting their records. As of this writing, the Federal Trade Commission (FTC) website for this info is: www.annualcreditreport.com.

Improving Your Score

If you want to improve your score, you'll need to think in terms of the components that comprise your score, as listed above. Improving your credit score is totally doable but it will take time. If you feel you need to improve this area of your life, you definitely can be successful, so long as you commit to the process and keep at it.

- Get current. Stay current. Pay your bills on time.
- Reduce your debt load. If you don't win the lottery, then pay down the smallest first.
- Reduce your revolving credit, or credit card balances. Get off of credit cards.
- Resolve any inaccuracies on your credit report. Be polite to the lenders you talk with on the phone...you catch more flies with honey...

Credit Counseling

While the use of credit counseling can hurt your credit score (because it shows lenders you are in a hardship situation), you should definitely use it if you need it. But, be careful! There are reputable firms and there are scoundrels out there. Learn about any firm you might use, before you engage them. A good place to get quality information is the National Federation of Credit Counseling (NFCC.org). This nonprofit can help you identify who can help you in your geographic area.

KEY TERMS

Credit Bureaus - Companies that gather and compile information used to derive credit scores. The main ones in the US are Transunion, Equifax, and Experion.

Credit CARD Act of 2009 - A federal statute passed in the spring of 2009 in response to what was seen at the time as gross overreaching and abuse by the US financial system. The main goals of the act were to improve transparency and to limit what were identified as abuses, such as the practice of universal default and exorbitant bank fees. Several unfair practices were corrected as a result of this act, but of course many loopholes remain, in spite of Congress's compromised scrutiny.

Credit Score - In order for a potential lender to determine the likelihood that you'd pay them back, a system of evaluating a borrower's creditworthiness developed over the years.

Creditworthiness basically concerns an evaluation about how good you might be at paying off your loans on time and in full. Most people in the US, sometime during their late teenage years to early twenties, begin to establish evidence of their creditworthiness (called a credit history).   You, without even knowing it, have left behind you a trail of evidence as to your credit worthiness.   There are three credit bureaus that gather and compile this type of information. These three bureaus are Equifax, Experian, and TransUnion.   Then, the Fair Isaac Corporation uses this info to create a number that lenders (such as banks, credit card issuers and the like) use to evaluate your credit risk. This score is called your FICO score.

Credit Union - Unlike a traditional neighborhood bank, and especially in contrast to the behemoth banking conglomerates that developed during the 1990s, credit unions are cooperatives that are owned and controlled by the people who use them. Used to be you'd mainly see credit unions serving finite communities such as federal employees, members of an association, or military personnel. Nowadays, many credit unions are gaining popularity as alternatives to local branches of banks. Credit unions offer most, if not all, of the services traditionally offered by banks. After the banking collapse of 2008—2011, many individual banking customers decided they feel more comfortable dealing with local organizations like credit unions, that seem more committed to the local retail customer.

Equity Loan/Equity Line of Credit - For purposes of this chapter, this is a type of loan (offered by banks and credit unions) that is based on the equity in one's real estate property. Because the loan is backed by property or "collateral" it typically carries a lower interest rate than unsecured consumer debt, like credit cards. Also, in some cases, such as when the equity loan is used to pay for renovations to the home, the interest rate may be tax deductible. This type of loan comes in a lump sum check paid to the borrower, which is somewhat different from an Equity Line of Credit. The Equity Line is similar, except that instead of receiving the approved loan amount as a lump sum check, the borrower receives a checkbook and can write checks up to the approved amount of the loan. This is more flexible, but may or may not be tax deductible, depending upon usage of the loan.

Leverage - In finance terms, this means exactly the same as debt or a loan. Credit also means the same thing. A credit card is a debt card...but they'd never get us to use them if we thought of them that way, now would they?

Interest: Compound and Simple - Simple Interest is when the rate is calculated on the same base, every year. So, if you have (or owe) $1,000, the simple interest of 5% on that is $1,000 multiplied by 5%, or $50 per year. It's the same every year: if the base amount is $1000, and the interest rate is 5%, then you earn (or owe) $50 every year.

With Compound Interest, the interest is calculated on a base that accumulates (or compounds) each period, say each year. So, the amount you earn (or owe) each year increases. Using compound interest on our example above, with the same $1,000 base and 5% rate, in year one the 5% is calculated on the base of $1,000, which equals $50. No change there. In year two, that $50 is added to the base, so the same 5% interest is calculated on a base of $1,050. This means the amount you earn (or owe) is now $52.50. In year three, this is added to the base so the same 5% interest is calculated using $1,102.50 as a base. 5% times $1,102.50 equals $55.125.

Note: interest can be divided up and calculated daily, weekly monthly, annually, depending on the particular situation. We don't go into that level of detail here. For now, we're just introducing the basic concept. So, for you math wonks out there who want to argue about when the rate is charged and what is the difference between current yield and yield to maturity, you'll have to wait until we write the chapter on fixed income securities.

Principal - This is the amount of an outstanding loan that has not yet been paid off.

Transunion, Equifax, and Experion - The three major US credit bureaus.

Universal Default - A misunderstood and unpopular tactic in the consumer lending industry during the 1990s and early 2000s. Under this widespread practice, a consumer's behavior in one credit contract could be used to change terms in all other areas. For example, if a consumer defaulted or became otherwise delinquent in one contract (say, a department store card), then issuers for all the other credit cards owned by that consumer could respond. Responses included greatly raised rates, fees, even cancellation. This was very unpopular due to its seeming insidiousness. Also, consumers rarely received obvious notice from issuers that their rates were being changed (no phone calls, just higher expenses). After much lobbying and complaint, this practice was largely curtailed through the Credit Card Accountability and Disclosure Act of 2009, or the Credit CARD Act. Of course, not all elements of universal default were repealed. Issuers can still cancel your card if you default in another area of your financial life...so read the fine print, and make polite but assertive phone calls.

CHAPTER SIX - THE ARTIST COLLABORATIVE, A GOOD IDEA?

Key Chapter Lessons:
1. Making money decisions by committee.
2. Different opinions, different views.
3. Taking the best of what each can offer.

Case Study: Art School Afterlife

Back when you were just coming out of art school, you knew to keep your eyes open. You watched your friends, tried to understand their decisions, wondered what might work for you. For example, take the question of where to live. You knew you weren't likely to make much money as a young unknown artist. So you'd have to set up your life such that you could afford a place to sleep, a studio to work in, and time to make it all happen.

An artist co-op was something that your friends talked about. Sounded like an interesting idea. A great way to learn the art biz. Something you should try.

Lucky for you, before you tried this yourself, a group of your pals launched just such a venture. Five of them came together to form a co-op in one of the old factory sites a couple of miles from downtown Providence, RI. They came up with the idea one night when they were all hanging around drinking beer.

They planned to live together, share studio space, and host art shows to help each other sell their work. They asked you to join them, but you bowed out. You wanted to see how it all played out first.

They called their cooperative...

ART SCHOOL AFTERLIFE

Great name, huh?

Art Show Number One: The Smashing Success?

About a month after establishing themselves in the old mill building, they hosted their first show. They invited all their friends. You went. Had a great time. Consumed much diet cola and BBQ corn chips while sitting too close to the bonfire out back (a gastronomically bad idea). Ended up going home without saying goodbye.

Next day, you woke feeling better and wanted to know how the show went. You assumed all went well. It was a simple enough undertaking, right? Just arrange some finished pieces on some tables. Throw up some partitions and tablecloths and voila! Instant gallery. Plus, from what you remember, everyone seemed to have a good time.

You heard from others who'd been there that the show was a smashing success. There were indeed many people in attendance and much art was sold. A few monied art patrons up from New York showed up.

Sounds impressive!

As soon as you arrived at the co-op, from the looks on your friends' faces, you could tell that all was not well. They were all still cleaning up. You couldn't quite put your finger on it, but it just seemed like there was...what's the word...discord in the atmosphere.

You talked with each of them as they worked.

Syd - "I dunno. Seemed fine to me. I sold some work...to my parents, which doesn't really count I guess. But, it's nice of them to support me. They've always supported my work, and I really appreciate them. I almost sold a big piece, a painted brick, to one of those guys from New York— or at least he was looking at it for such a long time that I felt sure he was about to buy. I might have  scared him off a little bit, when I stood too close to him. I was just, I dunno, kind of excited and didn't want to let him get away. So I guess it was kind of my fault when I bumped him. I don't think he got hurt or anything...and the coffee won't really stain so much because his jacket was black."

Prudence - "What a complete disaster. I don't even know where to begin. From the initial planning all the way through, it was just one bumbling mistake after another. And don't even try to say that we should just chalk it up to rookie mistakes—because it was so bad we might never be able to pull off another one.

"The place was a total and complete mess. Everyone's supplies and crap were all just pushed back against the wall.

Nanci and I were the only ones that even came close to tidying up our workspaces.

"There was no plan whatsoever for how to handle customers. It was just: *Oh you want to buy something? Fine, good luck locating the artist who made it!* I mean, I know I lost at least three sales because I was busy covering for Nunzio, who went AWOL right before the show began, and still hasn't shown back up.

"And Syd! I could've killed him when he assaulted the New Yorker I'd invited. I worked for months to cultivate that relationship, only to have him practically mobbed by dear old Syd!

"Then, I find out while New York was cleaning coffee off his shoes, turns out, he only came up because he wanted to meet Art. Art Art Art. Everyone just *loves* Art. So New York gets his chance to talk with Art, gives him his business card, and then without so much as a goodbye to me, he's out the door and on the road back to the City. Meanwhile, Art was too baked to even register the importance of this meeting. So baked that he dropped the guy's business card and would have lost it if it wasn't for wholesome Nanci coming to the rescue once again by finding the card on the floor. Aaarghh! It just makes me crazy even thinking about it all!"

Nanci - "I'd say, given all that we had to do to get ready, it went off okay. I sold a small piece, but a sale nonetheless, to one of the people who came up from New York. That was really exciting for me because it was the first piece I've sold outside of my circle of family and friends. Most

of my work is sold through word of mouth to someone who either knows me or is only one degree of separation away. So I felt happy, all in all.

"We'll need to tighten things up a bit if we want to do future shows. We should have a price list or something, so that everyone would know what each other is selling. That way we can be more knowledgeable about each other's work, which will probably lead to more sales.

"Also, I was thinking we should have a collective bank account. Then we could use that account when we need to pay for common expenses. In this show, I know I spent some money buying wine and I also bought a new broom so we could sweep up before the show. I know others bought some things as well, but I don't really know how much others contributed. I just kind of trust that everyone's trying to be fair and will do the right thing.

Art - "That show was kind of a trip. I had a good time. Met some folks from some big gallery somewhere, which was cool. But I always get so nervous whenever anyone makes me talk

about myself. I don't even want to deal with it. I just wish I could make some paintings and then let the rest take care of itself. I know that's not really realistic, so I try to talk with people.

"But when they start giving me so much attention, I just kind of freeze up and get all self-conscious and keep forgetting stuff. I know everyone just thinks I'm stoned all the time...which isn't totally untrue, I guess. It's not really because of that that I close up in public. I just never liked talking about myself, but the older I get and the more people that hear about my paintings, the more I find myself backed up against the wall. I wish they'd just look at the paintings, because everything I want to say is right there, and I say it better in my paintings than I could ever say in words...if that makes any sense.

"Oh, and one other thing. I thought the high point was when Syd bounced around that jerk from New York. The guy was just such a weasel, kept asking me if I had anyone taking care of me, looking after my business, and that I need a business manager and he just happens to know all about the art business.

"I was about to throw up all over the guy, so I told him to go look at one of Syd's paintings, telling him it was one of mine, because I knew that'd get him to leave me alone, and it was like Syd read my mind and was just all over the guy until he drove him out of the show. It was outrageous. I loved it. Syd's my man."

Nunzio? He's not back yet. But, that's okay. They can bring him up to date whenever he arrives.

Art Show Aftermath

You end up staying overnight (and you're not tellin' where you slept). So you are there when, late the next morning everyone is finally awake and lucid, Nanci suggests that they all need to come together and talk about the show.

You hover in the background with your ninth cup of coffee as the others (well, four of them anyway) sit down together. Nanci sets the agenda.

"Let's each say what we think went well and what went badly during the show. Okay?" she says.

There are nods in agreement all around. Syd and Art start doing rock, paper, scissors and are having a great time until they realize that they are just playing between the two of them, which doesn't really answer the question of who should go first. So they try to modify the game into a four-way version, but become confused about how that will work logistically—especially since Prudence refuses to participate.

"Fine. I'll go first," says Prudence. No one dares try to stop her.

Prudence "I said before that I thought the show was almost a total disaster. Now that I've had time to think it over, I want to tell you why. We scared off the guys from New York, who may never return my phone calls ever again. We fumbled around each other, probably discouraging potential buyers because they were so confused by our haphazard layout. We have no information about what sales we did in fact make."

Art "Awww all of this talk about money and details and who pays for what just makes my head hurt. I didn't move out here so that I could start acting like an accountant. I just want to be with my friends and make some paintings. I really don't care about any of the money stuff. So long as there's enough to cover the rent, it's all cool with me. I mean, I know that that stuff is important. I just don't think like that. I've never thought like that and I can't see myself starting now."

Prudence looked at Art for a long time. Her face flushed, but she stayed quiet. It was as if she'd never thought of the show in quite this way, as if she'd never thought of her relationship with Art in quite this way. She opened her mouth to speak, when Syd stood up.

Syd "Yeah, I really had fun too. But...well... the main thing that was great about the... I haven't even told you guys yet... So what happened was, that gallery guy from New York? The one I spilled coffee all over? Well, he called me on his way back to the City. He said he was a huge fan of Art's and had only really come to see his work. Long story short, he says he loves my work and wants to work it into this show he's thinking of doing next fall. He said, well his wife said, that she thought my bumbling around was *unpretentious* which is fine with me, whatever they want to call it. So in all, I'm thrilled with the show."

Before Syd could get himself further confused, the other roommates launched into congratulations. Art whooped with joy. Nanci offered a high five. Prudence smiled.

Nanci "I had a great time too. I agree we need to tighten things up before the next show. I have a lot of ideas about what areas we need to fix, which, because I'm such a geek, I actually wrote down:

- How should we manage money that comes in from sales?
- We'll need some way to make sure we have all the money accounted for.
- Should it all go into a common bank account or should we each use our own?
- How do we handle expenses? Will everyone be able to sign checks? Just one person?
- Should we accept credit cards for sales? Should we get a common credit card for expenses?

Nunzio? You guessed it...he's still AWOL.

> **Questions to Think About:**
> 1. Talk, talk, talk. Is that really the best thing for co-op partners to do?
> 2. Should they divide tasks? Share tasks? Develop some sort of hierarchy?
> 3. A formal agreement between them would probably be overkill, right? How might they capture their agreement so that they all know what it is?
> 4. What issues haven't been discussed here?

JUST TELL ME HOW

Different viewpoints. Different opinions. Each of them valid. Clearly, the main topic here is communication. The only way for multiple people to work together successfully on anything, especially when money's involved, is to have lots and lots and lots of communication. Of course, working by committee can be vexing. You can often end up with crazy-seeming outcomes. But, if that's the only way to keep everyone happy, then maybe that's the best outcome that can be reached.

Let's see what our gang of five figured out when they worked together.

Another Bite at the Apple

Our group of roommates, to their credit, recognized the great potential that lies in their diversity. If they take the best of what they each have to offer, they'll be stronger than any one of them could be alone.

But how to do this? How can they combine their talents into something that will work to produce a stable enterprise? They don't want to create something more complex and confusing than what their no-planning approach gave them the first time around. How can they organize themselves in a way that is effective, yet simple?

The answer, once they discovered it, was obvious. They all apparently embraced their newfound approach. You watched with admiration, and some worry, as the next show approaches. You, too, feel yourself buzzing with excitement and anticipation.

Just what was their newfound approach?

Simple. Each of them offered one gift for the good of the group. They each selected something they had to offer. And, since what they each offered was a gift, the others, recipients of each gift, needed only to be grateful and to put each gift to its best use.

You're impressed. Only artists would come up with an idea as wacky as this. You knew it just might work.

Which of the five friends came up with this brilliant idea? Why, Nunzio, of course.

Nunzio "It was during my most recent travels that this idea came to me. I was at Cannes—the festival is such a homecoming for me, I never miss seeing my people there—and while I enjoyed the gathering of glitterati, I couldn't stop thinking of our little group and the

issues that befell us in the maiden launch of our art show. I received no fewer than twenty texts from you all collectively during the show (not counting the dozen or so from Syd that I think were not intended for me...). It was clear that we needed to bring together ourselves into a union of strength.

"As a European, this solution was, if I might say, much more available to me than for you Americans. You all know just how much I love Americans, but your individualism can sometimes become impedimentary.

"The gift I'll contribute? I pledge my network of relationships. But I cannot promise (may you all forgive me) that I will be in attendance for every show. But I can promise that I will promote each show among my international network of *patrones de las artes*. I won't just say it, I'll actually show you what I do.

"Now, I'd love to stay and hear from each of you, but I must leave. I am meeting some dear friends at a millennial eclipse party in the Scandinavian tundras. I'll be sure to make them my first solicitation for our venture. Ciao! Besos!"

Nanci "Wow. That is so awesome and generous, Nunzio! It will be so helpful to have his marketing knowledge and connections. You know, he actually doesn't need to be here to do any of that. So, I don't mind that he is off doing whatever he does.

"I really love this idea of each of us contributing a gift. For my part, I've decided to contribute my gift of organizing. I think for this show, I'll focus specifically on how to organize the money. I was thinking I'd ask Prudie to help me implement it on the day of the show. For now, here are my thoughts:

"*Pricing* - We each set our own pricing: whatever we think will sell. If we're unsure, we can ask each other for perspectives. Each piece of art will have one of these small white stickers on it, and we'll write the price on the sticker. I'll keep a list that has the artist, title of piece, and price. I'll email it to each of you, and we can print out some copies to hand out.

"*Sales* - Any one of us can sell any piece of art in the show. We just have to stick to the pricing on the list. If some patron commits to buying a piece, we put a blue sticker (one of these here) on the white pricing sticker so everyone knows what's been sold. Then, whoever is handling that sale can bring the patron over to the Money Table. We'll take shifts so we always have one of us sitting at the table (including Nunzio...if he's in town...). Once the patron has been delivered to the Money Table, the person who delivered them can go back to help other patrons. Whoever is working their shift at the Money Table will takeover from there.

"*Keeping Track of Transactions* - We'll need to be able to keep track of what got sold. So, we'll keep one master list of all artwork for sale. We can keep this list on a clipboard which at all times during the show will stay at the Money Table. Whenever something is sold, we'll follow these steps: take in the money and make change if we have to; write down the sale under the correct column (cash, check, or credit); then provide a receipt. Also, it's a good time to take down their email address, so we can invite them to other events. I got this book of receipts. It

makes two receipts when you write on it. One goes to the patron and the other we'll keep in a folder in the drawer of the Money Table. Then, at the end of the show, we can count up all the receipts and compare them with the number of sales recorded on the master list. We should

have the same number of receipts as entries on the master list.

"*Handling Money* - We'll accept cash, checks, and credit cards. Here's how we can handle each. For cash, we'll have a metal cash box that we will keep in the drawer behind the Money Table when we're not making a sale. We'll start out the show with $100 in fives and tens so that we can make change.

We'll ask for exact change, but will of course accept whatever, as long as there are no bills over twenties. We send someone to make a deposit of excess cash, every hour or so.

"For checks, we'll just have to trust that people won't bounce them. Just to be sure, we can ask them to write their phone number on each check. We can also ask to see everyone's ID. We can run a photocopy of each ID and keep these in a separate folder in the Money Desk.

"For credit card sales, I know it's tempting to use one of the neat apps out there. But, I suggest we do it "manually" for this show. We'll get a better sense of how the system works, and then we can select parts of the process to automate later. To do this, we'll have to set up an account with some local bank branch.

"All the money taken in, whether from cash, check or card, will go into a common account I opened at the credit union. I opened this account as a joint checking account in each of our names. That way, we all have equal ownership. We can elect two of us to have signing authority on checks. Even if someone has ability to sign checks, they can only sign what everyone has already agreed to.

"*Payout From the Sales* - Because we all agreed to operate as a cooperative, I propose that we use a 70/30 split of proceeds from all sales made at the show. So, any artist gets 70% of the gross proceeds from whatever is sold of their artwork. The day after the show, when all the receipts have been tied out against the master list, checks will be cut from our common bank account for the amounts owed to each artist. We don't need to post a list of who made what (so we don't all have to feel jealous of the gobs of money Art's going to make). For the sake of transparency, and because we are all joint owners on the checking account, anyone can see who got paid what at any time.

"30% of gross proceeds stays in the checking account. That is the money that we will review each week and decide what we need to spend it on. Since it is common money, it has to go to a common need, like cleaning supplies for the studios or maintenance and repairs."

Prudence "I have to say that I approached our discussions with, well, skepticism. I have always been someone who only liked to rely on myself and my own talents. I have learned a lot from you all. The idea that we all contribute individual parts to help make a stronger whole is more than just touchy-feely...it's sensible. For once I don't want to be my bossy old self (oh come *on*... I know that's what you all think of me!). I want to pitch in.

"So. My gift to the group will be that I'll use my attention to detail (and my bossiness!) to make sure we see through all of our plans. I'll make sure the gallery is set up in a way that will be ready for patrons. Also, I'll take first shift at the Money Table so I can really learn the process Nanci sets up. Then, I'll keep checking in with others during their shifts to see if they have any questions, *and* to make sure we're all doing things the right way....

Syd "I agree with Pru. It's amazing: all the thinking you guys have done about this. I have to admit, I haven't really thought much about it since our last discussion. It all seems so strange to me. I'd be just as happy living in the woods somewhere, playing with puppets, like those brick puppets that I do a show with? But I want to do my part.

"I know everyone thinks I'm too busy partying to have much to offer. I think this is exactly the gift I want to contribute. No... I'm not going to try to get all the patrons drunk—not that I couldn't do it.

"But seriously, my gift is that I'm personable. Somewhere along the line when I was growing up, I developed a knack for making people relax and have a good time. Basically, if I like them, they like me.

"So for the show, I'll act as a kind of host. I won't be overbearing, that's not my style. I'll welcome people, see what they need, what they're looking for, and make sure they know what to do and where to go if they want to talk to one of the artists or make a purchase. I'll just make sure everyone is having a good time."

Art "Okay. So I've been thinking that I'm kind of the odd one out in all of this art show talk because I hate talking about art (especially mine) and I don't really give a shit if I sell any of it. But, for whatever reason, gallery people keep wanting to buy my work.

"I don't want to sound arrogant, so forgive me, but we've all talked about how sometimes people come and pay a lot, *a lot*, for my paintings. And I don't ever spend money on anything. I mean I buy everything I wear from Goodwill—I haven't gotten new clothes since my mom last took me back-to-school shopping in, like, fifth grade.

"That got me thinking about my gift to the group. So, for this show, and each show we do from here on out, I'll give money from the biggest piece I sell at the show. So, when the normal split is 70% to the artist and 30% to the common good, for the biggest piece I sell, I'll do the opposite: I'll only take 30% and the 70% can go to our common account.

"I hope that helps."

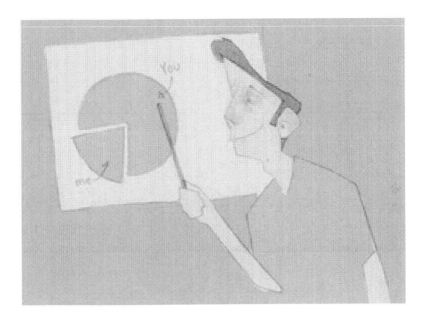

It does help. A lot.

On the day of the second show, you are at the cooperative with the others. You all share a sense of excitement when Prudence finally opens the doors. A crowd had gathered outside. They stream in and happily, you recognize only a few. This means all new patrons are coming, people beyond the original circle of family and friends.

"Thank you Nunzio," Prudence says with a smile as she watches the crowds of people gather around the various displays.

She said it aloud to herself, or to any roommates within earshot, or to no one at all. She can't say it to Nunzio because he, of course, is away on a cruise.

As luck would have it, you and the four remaining roommates hear her words. You all look at each other. Then, with great theatricality, you all pretend to search for the missing Nunzio. Then you all burst into laughter.

The four roommates turn to their responsibilities for the day. You watch them, happy that things seem to be going so well.

Teamwork. What an ordinary concept. But, for now, it seems to work.

KEY CONCEPT

Learn from your mistakes, talk to each other, build on your collective strengths. What you do together will be better than what you build alone, though the committee process can be a royal pain.

CHAPTER SEVEN - THE DARK ALCHEMY OF INVESTING

Key Chapter Lessons:
- Just what is investing anyway?
- Have you heard about the liquidity spectrum?
- What's the difference between asset allocation and diversification?
- How are you supposed to get money to invest in the first place?
- How and where can you go to make actual investments?
- Basic concepts in the world of investing.

Wall Street is a scam. A Ponzi scheme, a house of cards, a government-subsidised casino where you are swindled out of your honestly earned bucks by the giggling numerati.

Or...

Our global system of capital formation is a highly complex and sophisticated processor of information that can correctly evaluate the present and forecast the future.

Which of these characterizations is accurate? Take your pick. Both sound tempting, but in our humble opinion, it's sometimes hard to know which is more correct.

But y'know? After all is said and done, it's *our* Ponzi-scam-house-of-cards-information-processor. And so, as a member of this great ol' nation of ours, a little land I like to call...my country, you should really understand something about how this investing thing works. And, if you ever want to accumulate any monetary wealth at all, even a little, you'll need to know the basics.

In this chapter, we break the pattern of other chapters a bit (and why not? It's always good to mix things up). Instead of case study, we pose questions.

So What is Investing Anyway?

Say the word "investing" and people offer all sorts of disjointed commentary about **stocks** or **bonds** or **mutual funds** or **IRA**s or online trading accounts. Or they start squawking out their opinions about the ethics of Wall Street brokers. Or they talk with awe and jealousy about someone they know who bought some company's stock and then forgot about it, only to find out years later that they had become a billionaire. Or they simply love or hate the **annuity** they bought. Stories, tall tales, and jargon. Just what's it all mean?

Stocks, bonds, and mutual funds are only one part of the world of investing. Broadly speaking, investing is about figuring out where to store any money you are trying to accumulate, so you might protect it, maybe even grow it, until you need it.

That's kind of a broad definition, right? How about something a little more concrete?

A helpful starting point is a lil' thing we like to call the liquidity spectrum. Basically, **liquidity** deals with how easy it is to convert an asset to cash. If it's easy to turn into cash, the asset is considered liquid. If it's not easy to convert to cash, the asset is **illiquid**. See the liquidity spectrum graphic below:

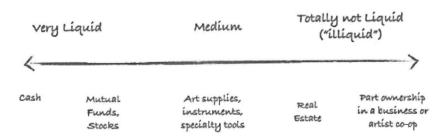

Time is Money? How?

It is as important to think about *when* you will need your money as it is to know *what* you'll need it for. If you have some money stashed away, and you might need ready access to it at any moment, then it has to be invested (stored) in a highly liquid form, such as cash. Cash won't grow much, if at all. It won't lose value either. And you can get to it when you need it.

A savings account is an example of an investment that's all in cash.

Do you need access to your money next week? Or can you set it aside for many years, even decades? These questions deal with the concept of the **Investment Time Horizon**. Once you've figured out your Investment Time Horizon, you'll be ready to address your **Allocation Plan** and then you can think about **Diversification** issues.

So, the first step in investing is to decide when and how you want to access your money. You might need some money soon (for example, in case you have an emergency), some you might need in say five years (to pay for a new used car), some you might want to put aside for the long-term. The long-term might be ten years from now, or it might be more.

In the short-term, you need high liquidity and you should not take on too much investment risk. Short-term investments are things like savings accounts, short-term CDs, and accounts that invest in **money markets**.

Medium-term investments can take on a little more risk, and can be a little less liquid. Short and intermediate term bonds and **US T Bills** and **Treasuries** are an example of this. Also conservative mutual funds (with no or very small sales expenses) can be a good alternative too.

Longer term investments can withstand the ups and downs of the markets over time, so the use of a full range of stocks, bonds, and other investments becomes possible.

Speaking of long-term, you really should put money away for when you're old and want to retire. Of course we're not talking about when you retire as an artist, you'll never retire from that! We're talking about the moment when you finally decide to hang up your career as a: dishwasher, security guard, waiter, janitor, art teacher, etc.

Once you've made decisions about time horizon (you could earmark different chunks of money for different spots on your time horizon), then you can consider the next key topic: your asset allocation plan.

What's an Allocation Plan?

Your allocation plan will have more impact on the performance of your investments than any other decision. For example, suppose you have an account that can hold any kind of investment (cash, **bonds**, **stocks**, **mutual funds**, etc.). This would be called a **brokerage account**. If you put 99% of the account into cash and the rest into one super risky stock, even if that stock doubles in value or plunges to zero, will it have a big effect on the overall value of the account? No.

Basic allocation is not a complex concept. You divide your account into different investment categories. The broad categories are cash, bonds, and stocks. You could include things like real estate investments and precious metals, but for now let's just keep it to cash, bonds, and stocks.

Each of these categories behave differently; each has a different level of risk and volatility; you could expect a different rate of return from each. Working together, these categories can provide a smoother and more predictable rate of return over the long run than you could expect from any one category alone.

You put a portion of your account into each category. The more you allocate toward the conservative end of the spectrum, the more conservative is the overall account. Vice versa for aggressive. This way, using allocation you can make the overall account conservative, moderate, or aggressive, depending upon the mix of investments you decide to use. It's not a foolproof strategy, but it's an important step.

To help you think about these categories, it's good to consider them as arrayed across a spectrum. Call it the risk/return spectrum. Low risk equals low return. High risk *may* equal high return (we say "may" because high risk may also mean losing money, which is why they call it high risk).

Allocation Rule of Thumb

How do you decide whether you want a conservative, moderate, or aggressive allocation plan? A good rule of thumb is to put the same percentage into conservative investments as the decade of life you're in. So if you're in your thirties, have 30% in conservative (bonds and cash), 70% in growth (stocks). In your fifties, you should be half and half: 50% conservative, 50% growth. And so on. This will help you grow your money through the years, and keep you out of trouble when you near retirement. Don't worry about trying to make your allocation plan too precise, keep it simple.

What should you do within each of these allocation categories? That's diversification. The next section addresses this question.

The Diversification Plan

You've probably heard the old truism that you shouldn't put all your eggs in one basket, right? Well, that truism refers to the idea of diversification. It is important to diversify in many different ways. We like to think of allocation as distributing your money across the categories of the risk/return spectrum. Diversification is how you spread about your money *within* these categories. It's like allocation is a macro decision and diversification involves micro decisions.

This is important. Remember 2008 and 2009? As that collapse showed, no one knows quite what is going to happen. So be prepared.

Diversifying your Conservative Allocation: When interest rates are low, it's a good idea to be patient and use a short-term bond mutual fund and leave some of your money in cash or money markets. When rates go up, it's a good idea to gradually move your bond fund investments toward a mix short-, medium-, and long-term bond funds, or find a fund that does this blend for you. Make sure your fund invests in high quality bonds: you could use a fund that contains a combination of US government bonds and highly rated corporate bonds. Sometimes people refer to bonds and bond funds as **fixed income**. In investing, fixed income investments is a broad category that includes bonds and other income-bearing investments.

Note, bonds are not without risk. The riskiness of a bond or bond fund is based on the maturity and quality of the bond. In bond funds, look at **average maturity** and **duration** to gauge a bond fund's riskiness. Lower maturity and duration mean lower risk, and lower return.

To assess the quality of a bond (or of bonds in a bond fund), consider whether you are investing in **high grade bonds** or **high yield bonds**. High grade bonds are highly rated and are considered low risk. The term "high yield bond" is Wall Street's euphemism for low grade or **junk bonds**, which, as the name implies are more risky. All can play a role. It's not like high grade is good and high yield is bad. Just know what you are using and why. If you want to be conservative, stick to high grade. Add in a small amount of high yield (or junk bonds) to get more income, at a higher level of risk.

Diversify Your Growth Allocation: Instead of trying to pick stocks on your own, you are likely to have better results if you use mutual funds. Use mutual funds that focus on stock investments, also known as **equities**. Equities are inevitably more volatile and risky than fixed income. Historically we thought of large companies as more stable and less volatile than small companies. This is still usually true, though not always. Many large companies, once considered safe long-term investments, can one day fall on hard times. Consider Citigroup, AIG, General Motors, and Kodak.

In general, if you use mutual funds to invest in equities, you can contribute more to large company stock funds (often called large cap funds), and less to small caps. **Capitalization** refers to the size of the company. Maybe split your stock allocation into thirds. Two-thirds can go to large cap funds. One-third can be split between small caps and international.

So How, Exactly, Do You Get Money to Invest?

Sure, you say. It's great to read all this investment stuff. But what if you aren't a trust fund baby, or you don't work for the next Google, or you won't inherit Daddy's firm, or you haven't sold the new world-changing masterpiece? What are you supposed to do then?

You'll have to do what other hardworking, decent, honest people do. You'll have to save your money.

If you say you can't save or invest because you think you're too _____ (fill in the blank: too young to worry about it, too old to start now, too poor, way too disorganized, etc.), then just hold on there a minute. No matter what your excuse, with care and planning, you can find a way to save money. In fact you must find a way. If you ever want to have any money, you'll need to put some away.

There's really no secret magic bullet. Most people who have money accumulated it by saving a little bit at a time, every month, for a long time. Get in the habit of saving, each month, for the rest of your life.

Don't rely on your own good will and determination. There are several ways to do this so it actually happens. If you have a job that has a **retirement plan**, you can have a bit deducted from each paycheck. If you are self-employed, like many artists and creatives, then you can set up a monthly deduction from your bank account—this monthly deduction can go into a savings account or into an IRA. There are other options out there. Choose what you understand and what makes the most sense to you. Just make sure you're saving.

Start Small, Try This Savings Tip:

If you think you can't save money, try the gradual approach. It works! Just stick with it, month after month, year after year. But be warned. Setting this up will require you to speak with someone who works at a bank, credit union, or brokerage firm. Don't worry. You'll find someone you can stand talking to about this. Just see it through. It will work.

1. Set up an automated monthly transfer (called and **ACH Transfer**) that goes from your checking account or from your paycheck into...

2. This monthly transfer goes into an account you can't access easily (no checkbook or debit card attached to it). It could be savings account, your employer's retirement plan, an **IRA**, or a brokerage account.

3. Begin with a small amount: Maybe you can only afford $15—$30 each month, that's fine. Contribute more if you can. Just make it an automated transfer (so you don't have to think about it).

4. Go out and live your life.

5. After 6 months, increase the monthly amount a bit, by $5 —$10. More if you can.

6. Go live your life.

7. At each 6 month interval, ratchet up the monthly amount you're putting away.

8. Doing it this way, you'll adjust your spending and lifestyle in such a way that you won't feel the pinch of saving.

9. When you get to 10% of your income, you can ease off the increases. Or keep going, but don't lock it all up, you'll need some access to that money sometime!

Where and How Do You Actually Invest?

But how, you may ask, do you actually make an investment? Where do you go? What will you need to deal with?

Well, that depends. If you have a retirement plan at work (assuming you have a job...), then you'll create an allocation plan and make investments within your plan. The plan will offer you a limited number of funds to choose from, and they're often presented in categories: stock funds, fixed income, etc. The human resources person at your workplace should have information about how open an account and get started.

If you don't have access to a retirement plan, then you can open your own doggone account (either an IRA of some sort or a taxable brokerage account). You'll need to decide how much handholding you want or need.

Do-it-yourself: Open an account at a firm that provides discount brokerage services. This does not mean that you're signing up to become a day trader. It means you're going to do the work primarily on your own, using the resources you find at the firm you choose, and in print and online. With this approach, you'll have lower transaction costs and cheaper mutual funds. These cost savings can really add up over time. But you'll be doing things on your own, which for some people is best and for others not so much.

Work with an Advisor: If you want to have an actual person that you can know and call on the phone to help you with this process, then you'll have to find a fit with one of the buh-zillions of financial brokers, advisors, planners, and consultants out there. The best scenario is to find a person with whom you can establish a long-term working relationship. They should take into account your total picture, not just your investments. They should be willing to take the time you need. They should make sure you understand things, such as how all the costs work, how they get paid, what are the different fees involved. To find the right fit, meet people in different parts of this field: one that works for a local branch of a big firm; one who works at a bank; one who is independent. Ask questions. Stay away from annuities if you don't understand them. Take your time. Then go with your gut. You can always change if you have to. You'll spend a bit more than the DIY person (maybe 1% of total assets is fair). But it could be money well spent.

That's It?

Of course there's more to it...or there can be. But it does not have to be alchemy. Keep it simple. Spend the next twenty or thirty years or more saving some money every month. Spread it out among different types of assets (real estate, cash, stock and bond mutual funds). Do this and you'll eventually end up well-prepared.

If you diversify your liquid investments among a blend of stock and bond mutual funds, you'll grow your money and protect it some, too.

Will you miss the next best investment to come along? Could you have done better if you had only thought to put more of your money into that thing that went up, and less into that thing that went down? Sure.

You'll always miss the best investments. And the worst ones. And you also won't be the one who bought the mega-millions lottery ticket either.

If you take your time, if you slowly grow and protect your money over many years. Ignore all the hype. Stick to your plan. Pay attention. Don't panic and don't get greedy.

You will end up with some money. Maybe even enough.

Questions to Think About:
1. What steps should you go through to make an investment game plan?
2. Should you have different accounts for different financial goals, or one account for everything?
3. True or false: working with an advisor is worse than doing it on your own?
4. What's more important in an investment, liquidity or volatility?
5. An IRA account should be used for long-term investing, why?

KEY TERMS

ACH Transfer - Automatic Clearing House transfers are electronic transfers of money. Once set up, they make transfers of cash very simple. Normally, if a transfer request is submitted before noon on a business day, the money will be in the receiving account on the following business day. Remember, if you make a request for an ACH transfer on a Friday of a long weekend (when a lot of people decide to make last minute financial transactions), and you miss the noon deadline, it could be that your transfer doesn't go through until Wednesday: you missed the noon deadline, so the transfer is implemented on the next business day, which is Tuesday; then the receiving gets the funds on the business day after that. People

Annuity - See all this text here about annuities? That's because they can be confusing and complex. They might be for you, but make sure you take the time to understand. An annuity is an investment product that has a lot of bells and whistles. There are two main classes of annuity: fixed and variable. Basically, you put money into an annuity and then you can't touch it for a while (like seven years or until you reach 59 and a half). The money grows and then when you go to take the money out, several years in the future, you pay income taxes on the amount growth. The basic gist of annuities is that they are investment vehicles with an insurance wrapper. What this means is that you get the benefits of investment (such as growth or income), but the insurance features can eliminate risk (of stock market collapse). Of course, you pay for these insurance features. Fixed annuities are safe. Variable annuities offer more growth because some of your money would be invested in the stock market. Since annuities can quickly become confusing, it can be helpful into divide your thinking about (especially variable) annuities into buckets: the death benefit (what your beneficiaries get if you die), the living benefit (what type of income stream you could turn your annuity into...there are usually several options), and the cash value (what the amount you invested is worth if you wanted to withdraw it, or take a distribution—i.e., what's left after growth, fees, penalties, etc.).

Bond - When a bond is issued by a corporation, government or municipality, you (the investor) are essentially making a loan to the issuer. But, from your perspective as an investor, a bond is something you can put your money into in order to achieve a (hopefully) safe and predictable return (or interest rate). The interest rate you receive for holding a bond varies depending upon two factors: the length of time you have to hold the bond until it comes due (this is called maturity, common maturities are one, five, ten, or twenty years), and whether or not the bond is risky (the quality). Some bonds are very safe investments (like the Treasuries issued by the US government). And some are mostly safe (like those issued by highly rated corporations). And some are risky (like those issued by companies or countries or municipalities with low credit ratings). There are credit rating agencies (such as Moody's or Standard & Poor) that are in the business of evaluating the creditworthiness of bond issuers. Usually these rating agencies do a good job, but they are paid by the issuers whom they rate. Conflict of interest? You betcha! So be careful. Safer is better, but nothing's fool proof.

Average Maturity - Within a bond mutual fund, that is, a mutual fund composed of bonds, average maturity is just what it sounds like: the average of all the maturities of bonds within the fund. This measure can give you a sense of interest rate risk and potential income for the fund. A lower average maturity usually means lower interest rate risk, and lower income. Remember, quality of bonds is also a factor in determining fixed income riskiness.

Brokerage Account - This is a standard investment account. It can hold a wide range of types of investments, from conservative (like money markets) to aggressive (like small cap stocks). It can hold individual securities (like individual stocks or bonds) or mutual funds. These accounts can be taxable or tax-advantaged (as in an IRA).

Capitalization - This is a measure of the overall size of a company. Put most simply, a company's capitalization is derived by taking all the company's stock and multiplying it by the stock price.

CD - Certificates of Deposit (CDs) are a lot like a super safe bond issued by a bank (see bond description above). Your investment is insured by the government (FDIC), so CDs are considered quite safe investments. And, because the quality is high, the rate of return you receive is lower than with a bond of the same maturity with a lower quality rating.

Commission - This is the fee a broker earns when he/she sells you a stock or mutual fund. These are almost always negotiable, so you should make sure to ask for the best price he/she can give you. And, ask twice, because they'll probably cave and give you a good deal. Commissions shouldn't drive your broker's decision to buy or sell. So, if you get a suggestion out of the blue from a broker to make a buy or sell decision, they should be able to convince you that it is truly an opportunity that is in your best interest. And, ask for a discount, twice, at least.

Duration - This is a very important measurement when considering a fixed income mutual fund (AKA a bond fund). Duration describes the fund's potential sensitivity to fluctuations in interest rates. The fund's duration number, expressed in years, is supposed to equate how much the fund's price will change in response to a one percent change in interest rates. So, if a fund's duration is 11 years, then a one percent increase in interest rates should mean the fund's value (NAV) will drop by 11%. Interest rates and bond prices have an inverse relationship on one another. As interest rates rise, bond funds go down in value. Vice versa if interest rates fall.

Equities - In investing, the term "equities" means exactly the same thing as stocks: stocks = equities. When investing in stocks, you are investing in a part ownership share in the equity of a company.

Expense Ratio - This is the metric for measuring the internal expenses that come embedded within a mutual fund. Basically, in order for a mutual fund to do what it does (see mutual fund description below), it incurs various expenses such as management, marketing, administration, and so on. Since these can be complex and difficult to track, the expense ratio is the measure that evolved so that individual investors can have a way to make apples to apples comparisons between funds. Actively managed funds have higher expense ratios, index funds have low expense ratios. While this metric is important, it should not be the only factor used in making a decision about a fund. An "expensive" fund might be in just the right sector or it might have excellent returns. Alternatively, an "inexpensive" fund might be the wrong place to put your money at this time. So you have to consider the expense ratio, along with other things (like long-term fund performance, volatility, income, etc.)

in order to decide if a given fund is a good or bad investment idea.

Fixed Income Investments - This is what the investment world uses to refer to securities, or investments, that provide an income stream for investors. Fixed income can refer to corporate bonds, US Treasury bonds, municipal bonds, and CDs. There are other securities that are like bonds and are considered fixed income, but aren't literally bonds, such as preferred stocks. Sometimes REITs are considered part of a fixed income portfolio. Interest rate fluctuations, and maturities & quality of individual securities, are the variables that determine riskiness of fixed income security.

High Grade Bonds - Rating agencies, such as Moody's, Fitch, and Standard & Poor, evaluate bonds issued by companies and government entities. They then rate these securities according to their quality. Each agency uses a slightly different rating scale and process, but most people know what is meant by a "triple A rated" company or government entity. A triple A rating is supposed to be the standard of excellence, and usually is. Remember that in 2008-2010, many companies and agencies with AAA ratings were discovered to have tremendous underlying financial problems. AIG, Freddie Mac, and Fannie Mae were all AAA rated at one point and now are poster children for corporate mismanagement. So, when assessing a bond, ratings are important but must be considered with some cynicism.

Illiquid - Not liquid, as in, an asset that is not easily converted to cash. Like a 10% ownership in your cousin's pizza shop. Might have some value, but you ain't never going to be able to sell that for cash...at least not soon.

Investment Time Horizon - The amount of time the investor can leave an investment alone, without disturbing it. It is important to consider this when choosing an investment strategy. Time horizon, plus the investor's willingness/ unwillingness to live with market volatility are key to determining the correct types of investments for an account. Don't put short-term investments in illiquid vehicles (like annuities) or risky securities (like internet high fliers).

IRA - This stands for "Individual Retirement Account." There are many different types of IRAs: some for small businesses and some for individuals. What each type of IRA has in common is that they are accounts that a person can put money from income into, and receive a tax benefit in return. For tax deferred accounts, money invested is then deducted from the contributor's income in the current year, so the contributor pays lower taxes in that year. Then, contributions can grow and no taxes are owed on the gains or income until distributions begin in retirement (indeed there are penalties if a person tries to take money out of a retirement account before age 59.5). When distributions occur in retirement, the account owner will have to add the distributions to their income, and pay income taxes on the total amount. ROTH IRAs are different in that contributions are made with after tax dollars, so there is no tax break in the year of the contribution. And, no taxes are owed when the account owner goes to take distributions in retirement. In summary, for a Traditional IRA, taxes are *deferred* until retirement. For a ROTH IRA, distributions in retirement are tax *free*.

Junk Bonds - These are low-grade fixed income investments. The rating agencies (see high grade definition above) assign a low rating to bonds from companies or agencies that are experiencing financial trouble. Since the term "junk bonds" has such a negative ring to it, Wall Street came up with the euphemism "high yield" to use instead. Junk bonds are called high yield bonds. These bonds need to offer a higher yield in order to entice investors to take on the higher level of risk. But, there can be a place for high yield/junk bonds in a fixed income portfolio. A small portion of high yield bonds provide a little extra income to an otherwise conservative portfolio. High yield means higher risk, but not definite risk. So adding this to a portfolio is a step that can be taken, but only with careful planning and expectations.

Liquidity - This refers to how easy it is to turn an investment into cash. Think spectrum. Some things that are really easy to turn into cash (like, well, cash) are highly liquid investments. Stocks and bonds and mutual funds are very liquid too, not quite as liquid as cash, but close. Just one call to your (super honest, open-minded, and attentive) broker and your holdings are turned into cash...for a small commission. Other assets are not liquid, or are less liquid. Real estate or part ownership in your brother's pizza shop are very illiquid assets. If you need cash tomorrow, try selling that 10% share of your brother's business, or that condo that's been on the market for almost a year.

Money Market Funds - These are technically mutual funds that contain highly liquid and safe investments. Money market funds comprise the cash portion of a brokerage account's asset allocation. They are composed of very short-term "near cash" investments, such as short-term CDs or bank notes. Typically, any cash that is uninvested in an investor's brokerage account is automatically swept into money market funds. They provide a safe place to park cash for a time, and a low rate of return. In 2009, even money market funds showed that during a collapse, nothing is completely safe. There were some money market funds that famously had to receive contributions from their parent companies to keep from "breaking the buck" or going negative. This had been unimaginable a few months prior.

Mutual Fund - This is an investment that you can put money into if you want an easy way to diversify your investment. Basically, if you have say $1000 to invest, it might be hard for you to diversify that investment...it'd be difficult to buy shares in 100 different companies with your one grand. Mutual funds do this for you. They take your one thousand dollars and pool it with many other investors, then with that larger pool of cash, they invest into a diversified portfolio. There are many types of mutual funds, from aggressive to conservative, from cheap index funds (which are only supposed to mirror the performance of a certain index, like the S&P 500) to actively managed funds (which, for a fee, employ supposedly smart people to make active trades in the fund in an effort to provide performance that is better than an index). Which fund is for you is a matter of preference and depends upon things like your age, how much risk you want, how sensitive you are to volatility and fees, etc.

Retirement Plan - There are many different types of retirement plans, but in essence, a retirement plan is something your employer has put in place that you can use to save for retirement. Different types include the 401(k), 403(b), pension plans, and so on. They typically have a lot of rules and guidelines, laid out by the government to protect participants (you) from employers that might seek sneaky ways to stash away money without paying taxes (not that that would *ever* happen). For participants (employees), these plans are generally a good thing. If you sign up to participate, and you should, your contributions are normally taken about of your paycheck and sent directly to your account at the plan. Also, you are sometimes given a match, which means that your employer puts away a certain amount into your account on your behalf (it's like getting a bonus: if you put away money—they put away some too). Retirement plans are an effective way to make sure you're saving money for your future. And if you ever leave your job, your retirement plan account is still yours. You can roll it into an IRA or transfer it into the plan of your next employer. There are a few more wrinkles and bells and whistles about retirement plans, but for now, that about explains them.

Sales Load - The term used to describe an expense charged to you when you buy certain mutual funds. There are many different share classes of mutual funds, and so there are many different sales loads. The term "sales load" sounds pretty negative, right? And sometimes, you might really be better off not using a fund that charges a sales load. But, this isn't the only criterion you should use in assessing a fund. If the fund is an excellent performer, seems it will do just what you need in a fund, has a long track record, and so on, it might be worth the fee to buy into it. Or it might not. Do some homework, make a decision based on several factors. Don't just look at this one factor. Index funds do not have sales loads, so are appealing to many people because they are cheaper. Generally, for large cap equity funds, you'd be better off with an index fund because few managers in this style can beat their index over a long period of time. But, with other styles on investing (foreign, small cap, high yield, etc.), active fund managers can often beat their index. So, maybe the best thing is to use a blend of index and active funds.

Stock - A stock is a part ownership in a company. Every company has a certain monetary value (or, each company is worth a certain amount of money). Say you figured out the value of a company. Divide this value into a number of equal parts (say a thousand parts, or a million). Then these parts, called "shares," can be sold to investors. Each investor becomes part owner of the company, according to the number of shares they bought. The company can use the proceeds from selling those shares to fund their business operations. Private companies sell shares to a small circle of investors. Public companies sell shares on open markets, called exchanges (such as the New York Stock Exchange or NASDAQ, there are many exchanges in the US and abroad). Once the company has sold (or "issued") shares to the public via an exchange, the shares are then traded among people based on whether an investor wants to hold or sell their shares. After a public company originally issues its shares on an exchange and has received proceeds from that action (call an offering, like an IPO), it doesn't receive any additional money when one investor sells its shares to another.

GLOSSARY

Compilation of terms and concepts from previous chapters.

Jim Bush

ACH Transfer - Automatic Clearing House transfers are electronic transfers of money. Once set up, they make transfers of cash very simple. Normally, if a transfer request is submitted before noon on a business day, the money will be in the receiving account on the following business day. Remember, if you make a request for an ACH transfer on a Friday of a long weekend (when a lot of people decide to make last minute financial transactions), and you miss the noon deadline, it could be that your transfer doesn't go through until Wednesday: you missed the noon deadline, so the transfer is implemented on the next business day, which is Tuesday; then the receiving gets the funds on the business day after that. People

Annuity - See all this text here about annuities? That's because they can be confusing and complex. They might be for you, but make sure you take the time to understand. An annuity is an investment product that has a lot of bells and whistles. There are two main classes of annuity: fixed and variable. Basically, you put money into an annuity and then you can't touch it for a while (like seven years or until you reach 59 and a half). The money grows and then when you go to take the money out, several years in the future, you pay income taxes on the amount growth. The basic gist of annuities is that they are investment vehicles with an insurance wrapper. What this means is that you get the benefits of investment (such as growth or income), but the insurance features can eliminate risk (of stock market collapse). Of course, you pay for these insurance features. Fixed annuities are safe. Variable annuities offer more growth because some of your money would be invested in the stock market. Since annuities can quickly become confusing, it can be helpful into divide your thinking about (especially variable) annuities into buckets: the death benefit (what your beneficiaries get if you die), the living benefit (what type of income stream you could turn your annuity into...there are usually several options), and the cash value (what the amount you invested is worth if you wanted to withdraw it, or take a distribution—i.e., what's left after growth, fees, penalties, etc.).

ARM - Adjustable Rate Mortgage, as in the rate you'd pay will change, adjust, over the term of the loan. Do you think it will adjust *down*? Hah! See Mortgages, Variable for more.

Average Maturity - Within a bond mutual fund, that is, a mutual fund composed of bonds, average maturity is just what it sounds like: the average of all the maturities of bonds within the fund. This measure can give you a sense of interest rate risk and potential income for the fund. A lower average maturity usually means lower interest rate risk, and lower income. Remember, quality of bonds is also a factor in determining fixed income riskiness.

Balance Sheet - This is one of the main statements used if you want to look at something from a financial perspective. If you're looking at a company or not for profit, the statement is called a Balance Sheet. If you're looking at an individual person, it's called a Statement of Net Worth. In either case, the statement provides a snapshot of where you or your business stand on a given date.

Bond - When a bond is issued by a corporation, government or municipality, you (as the investor) are essentially making a loan to the issuer. But, from your perspective as an investor, a bond is something you can put your money into in order to achieve a (hopefully) safe and predictable return (or interest rate). The interest rate you receive for holding a bond varies depending upon two factors: the length of time you have to hold the bond until it comes due (this is called maturity, common maturities are one, five, ten, or twenty years), and whether or not the bond is risky (the quality). Some bonds are very safe investments (like the Treasuries issued by the US government). And some are mostly safe (like those issued by highly rated corporations). And some are risky (like those issued by companies or countries or municipalities with low credit ratings). There are credit rating agencies (such as Moody's or Standard & Poor) that are in the business of evaluating the creditworthiness of bond issuers. Usually these rating agencies do a good job, but they are paid by the issuers whom they rate. Conflict of interest? You betcha! So be careful. Safer is better, but nothing's foolproof.

Brokerage Account - This is a standard investment account. Can hold a wide range of types of investments, from conservative (like money markets) to aggressive (like small cap stocks). Can hold individual securities (like individual stocks or bonds) or mutual funds. These accounts can be taxable or tax-advantaged (as in an IRA).

Capitalization - This is a measure of the overall size of a company. Put most simply, a company's capitalization is derived by taking all the company's stock and multiplying it by the stock price.

Cash Flow Statement - This helps you figure out the net difference between cash coming in from all sources, less cash going out. If the results are negative you have a deficit (like, say, the US government). There is a saying: "cash is king," which can probably mean different things in different settings. But in terms of cash flow, it means that you need to have enough money coming in regularly to pay your bills. If you have a big sum of money coming in soon (from say a grant or a commission), you might be rich when that money arrives, but if you can't pay your bills between now and then, you have a cash flow problem.

CD - Certificates of Deposit (CDs) are a lot like a super safe bond issued by a bank (see Bond description above). Your investment is insured by the government (FDIC), so CDs are considered quite safe investments. And, because the quality is high, the rate of return you receive is lower than with a bond of the same maturity with a lower quality rating.

Collateral - When a loan is secured by collateral, that means the lender will own the collateral if the borrower defaults. A house is the collateral on a mortgage. A car is the collateral on an auto loan. Unsecured loans have no collateral. Examples of this are credit cards, department store cards, or other forms of consumer debt. Since there is no collateral for the lender to seize if the borrower defaults on this loan, then the interest rates are usually higher.

Commission - This is the fee a broker earns when he/she sells you a stock or mutual fund. These are almost always negotiable, so you should make sure to ask for the best price he/she can give you. And, ask twice, because they'll probably cave and give you a good deal. Commissions shouldn't drive your broker's decision to buy or sell. So, if you get a suggestion out of the blue from a broker to make a buy or sell decision, they should be able to convince you that it is truly an opportunity that is in your best interest. And, ask for a discount, twice, at least.

CPA - Also known as an accountant, a CPA is a licensed professional who gets paid to keep you out of debtor's prison. Okay...not really. Or at least not any more. This term refers to a person who's taken and passed a very rigorous course of study to earn the designation "Certified Public Accountant." CPAs can work for big companies, banks, brokerage firms and so on. But most individuals interact with CPAs when they need help preparing and filing their taxes (whether personal or small business/not for profit). A good CPA understands the laws and regulations regarding taxes in the US. They can help you figure out what to do in various tax- and business-related situations. They also are often involved in companies helping to prepare audits and bookkeeping.

Credit Bureaus - Companies that gather and compile information used to derive credit scores. The main ones in the United States are Transunion, Equifax, and Experion. The Fair Isaac Corporation uses this info to create a number that lenders (such as banks, credit card issuers and the like) use to evaluate your credit risk. This score is called your FICO score.

Credit CARD Act of 2009 - A federal statute passed in the spring of 2009 in response to what was seen at the time as gross overreaching and abuse by the US financial system. The main goals of the act were to improve transparency and to limit what were identified as abuses, such as the practice of universal default and exorbitant bank fees. Several unfair practices were corrected as a result of this act, but of course many loopholes persevered congress's compromised scrutiny.

Credit Score - In order for a potential lender to decide whether you'll pay them back, a system of evaluating a borrower's creditworthiness developed over the years. Creditworthiness basically concerns an evaluation about how good you might be at paying off your loans on time and in full. Most people in the United States, sometime during their late teenage years to early twenties, begin to establish evidence of their creditworthiness (called a credit history). You, without even knowing it, have left behind you a trail of evidence as to your credit worthiness.

There are several things that matter in your credit score (or your FICO score). According to the www.myFICO.com website, 35% of your score is from your payment history (on things like rent, debt payments, cell phone payments), 30% is how much you owe, 15% is the length of your credit history, 10% is the amount of new credit, and 10% is the types of credit used. Remember credit means the same thing as loans or debt.

Credit Union - Unlike a traditional neighborhood bank, and especially in contrast to the behemoth banking conglomerates that developed during the 1990s, credit unions are cooperatives that are owned and controlled by the people who use them. Used to be you'd mainly see credit unions serving finite communities such as federal employees, members of an association, or military personnel. Nowadays, many credit unions are gaining popularity as alternatives to local branches of banks. Credit unions offer most, if not all, of the services traditionally offered by banks. After the banking collapse of 2008—2011, many individual banking customers decided they feel more comfortable dealing with local organizations like credit unions, that seem more committed to the local retail customer.

Debit Card - These are often confused with credit cards, but they behave differently. Many bank accounts (or other accounts where someone holds money) offer debit cards as a way to get money out of the account. When you purchase something with a debit card, the process looks and feels similar to using a credit card. You swipe your card and, instead of signing your name, you sometimes have to enter your PIN code. From then on, the item you purchased is yours.

Except what happens behind the scenes is different from credit. With a debit card, the amount of your transaction is deducted from your bank account. So if you buy something for $45 and you used you debit card, shortly after your transaction at the cashier or checkout (again, real or virtual), your account is reduced, or debited, $45.

This is handy because you don't have to carry around cash. And, you aren't charged interest because you're not taking a loan as with a credit card.

Though debit cards can be a great tool, there are two main problems with them, problems that aren't often talked about. First, there are fees that can arise that you might not know about (such as transaction fees, annual fees and getting whacked if you overdraw your account). The second problem is that people generally spend more when they use debit cards—a lot more. Retailers and banks know this. They're very good at separating you from your money. Carry cash and use that.

Deductions - You pay income taxes on, you guessed it, your income. The US Tax Code offers opportunities for tax filers to reduce the amount of income they have to pay taxes on. Basically, there are many items that the IRS has been asked to put into the Code as exemptions, things that enable a tax filer to reduce their taxable income. So for example if someone made $50,000 per year in income and had $10,000 in deductions, they'd have *taxable income* of $40,000. How are these deductions determined? Well, the best way to understand that is to know that deductions come through the political system (Federal, state, and local). So if politicians want to encourage one sort of behavior in individuals, they can offer a deduction as an incentive. The cynics among us will say that politicians also create deductions as a way to "pay off" their rich corporate campaign contributors...but we'd never be that cynical, right? Since the Tax Code is a product of the political process, how many guesses you want to make about whether it holds up as a logical, un-contradictory document? Okay, one guess, you get one guess.

Duration - This is a very important measurement when considering a fixed income mutual fund (AKA a bond fund). Duration describes the fund's potential sensitivity to fluctuations in interest rates. The fund's duration number, expressed in years, is supposed to equate how much the fund's price will change in response to a one percent change in interest rates. So, if a fund's duration is 11 years, then a one percent increase in interest rates should mean the fund's value (NAV) will drop by 11%. Interest rates and bond prices have an inverse relationship on one another. As interest rates rise, bond funds go down in value. Vice versa if interest rates fall.

Equities - In investing, the term "equities" means exactly the same thing as stocks: stocks = equities. When investing in stocks, you are investing in a part ownership share in the equity of a company.

Equity Loan/Equity Line of Credit - This is a type of loan (offered by banks and credit unions) that is based on the equity in one's real estate property. Because the loan is backed by property or "collateral" it typically carries a lower interest rate than unsecured consumer debt, like credit cards. Also, in some cases, such as when the equity loan is used to pay for renovations to the home, the interest rate may be tax deductible. This type of loan comes in a lump sum check paid to the borrower, which is somewhat different from an Equity Line of Credit. The Equity Line is similar, except that instead of receiving the approved loan amount as a lump sum check, the borrower receives a checkbook and can write checks up to the approved amount of the loan. This is more flexible, but may or may not be tax deductible, depending upon usage of the loan.

Estimated Taxes - If you are a sole proprietor, you do not have taxes withheld from your pay. You still have to pay, but need to manage the tax payments yourself and there are penalties for underpayment. Your estimated taxes are intended to cover your liability from *self-employment tax* as well as state and federal income taxes. You typically pay estimated taxes on a quarterly basis.

Expense Ratio - This is the metric for measuring the internal expenses that come embedded within a mutual fund. Basically, in order for a mutual fund to do what it does (see mutual fund description below), it incurs various expenses such as management, marketing, administration, and so on. Since these can be complex and difficult to track, the expense ratio is the measure that evolved so that individual investors can have a way to make apples to apples comparisons between funds. Actively managed funds have higher expense ratios, index funds have low expense ratios. While this metric is important, it should be the only factor used in making a decision about a fund. An "expensive" fund might be in just the right sector or it might have excellent returns. Alternatively, an "inexpensive" fund might be the wrong place to put your money at this time. So you have to consider the expense ratio, along with other things (like long-term fund performance, volatility, income, etc.)

in order to decide if a given fund is a good or bad investment idea.

Extensions - For tax filing, sometimes a person or company can't get their taxes done and filed by the required date (mid April for individuals). If this happens, the IRS permits you to request an extension, which gives you permission to file a few months later. Use this option if you really have to; it's better to file an extension than to file late, incomplete, or incorrectly. Don't use this if you're just lazy and a procrastinator. In most cases, just get your taxes done and filed on time, and then move on with your life.

Fixed Income Investments - This is what the investment world uses to refer to securities, or investments, that provide an income stream for investors. Fixed income can refer to corporate bonds, US Treasury bonds, municipal bonds, and CDs. There are other securities that are like bonds and are considered fixed income, but aren't literally bonds, such as preferred stocks. Interest rate fluctuations, and maturities & quality of individual securities, are the variables that determine riskiness of fixed income security.

Grant - Money given to an applicant to be used as specified in the application. So, if you get a grant to, say, build a super cool installation outside a library, don't use that grant money to go visit friends in Ohio! Use the money as intended: a well meaning gift that is intended to support your work.

Grant Cycle - Grant making organizations often operate on an annual cycle. They accept submissions up to a certain date; review them for a period of time; and they make decisions and notify applicants after a certain date. Then, the next year, they do it all again. Note that they may have just one major application deadline each year; or they may have several different deadlines. But then, of course you'll have this all figured out because you'll read their submission guidelines.

Grant Making Organizations - These are, as the name implies, organizations that give out grant money. They might be private foundations (where some rich person sets up a fund to be used to make grants toward particular needs). Or they might be parts of big corporations (often called something like the charitable giving department). Or government agencies (like a local arts or humanities council). They usually focus their giving on specific areas: arts, poverty, education, and so on. You know...things that no one makes money doing, but they do them anyway because the work is worthy and needs to be done.

Grantees - These are the people seeking grants. Also called applicants, or starving artists.

Grants Officer - This is the person within a grant making organization that administers the grants process. They publicize their organization's grant process and cycle, work with applicants during and after the grant process is complete, and they notify applicants of whether their application got accepted or rejected. They also may provide field support, such as setting up workshops or helping grantees comply with grant guidelines. They are usually great people to know and work with! But don't expect that they are the ones that make the yes/ no decisions. Most organizations consider grant applications through a committee process.

High Grade Bonds - Rating agencies, such as Moody's, Fitch, and Standard & Poor, evaluate bonds issued by companies and government entities. They then rate these securities according to their quality. Each agency uses a slightly different rating scale and process, but most people know what is meant by a triple A rated company (or government entity). A triple A rating is supposed to be the standard of excellence, and usually is. Remember that in 2008-2010, many companies and agencies with AAA ratings were discovered to have tremendous underlying financial problems. AIG, Freddie Mac, and Fannie Mae were all AAA rated at one point and now are poster children for corporate mismanagement. So, when assessing a bond, ratings are important but must be considered with some cynicism.

Illiquid - Not liquid, as in, an asset that is not easily converted to cash. Like a 10% ownership in your cousin's pizza shop. Might have some value, but you ain't never going to be able to sell that for cash...at least not soon.

Income Statement - This helps you track earnings less expenses for a given period, itemized by category. We also here refer to it as the Income and Expense Worksheet, because developing one of these for yourself or for an organization is an important step in developing a budget.

Independent Contractor - You get paid for a job and there are no payroll taxes taken out. Makes you a sole proprietor by default, and subject to self-employment tax.

Interest Rate (Compound and Simple) - Simple interest is when the rate is calculated on the same base, every year. So, if you have (or owe) $1,000, the simple interest of 5% on that is $1,000 times 5%, or $50 per year. It's the same every year: if the base amount is $1000, and the interest rate is 5%, then you earn (or owe) $50 every year.

With Compound Interest, the interest is calculated on a base that accumulates (or compounds) each period, say each year. So, the amount you earn (or owe) each year increases. Using compound interest on our example above, with the same $1,000 base and 5% rate, in year one the 5% is calculated on the base of $1,000, which equals $50. No change there. In year two, that $50 is added to the base, so the same 5% interest is calculated on a base of $1,050. This means the amount you earn (or owe) is now $52.50. In year three, this is added to the base so the same 5% interest is calculated using $1,102.50 as a base. 5% times $1,102.50 equals $55.125.

Note: interest can be divided up and calculated daily, weekly monthly, annually, depending on the particular situation. We don't go into that level of detail here. For now, we're just introducing the basic concept. So, for you math wonks out there who want to argue about when the rate is charged and what is the difference between current yield and yield to maturity, you'll have to wait until we write the chapter on fixed income securities.

Investment Time Horizon - The amount of time the investor can leave an investment alone, without disturbing it. It is important to consider this when choosing an investment strategy. Time horizon, plus the investor's willingness/ unwillingness to live with market volatility are key to determining the correct types of investments for an account. Don't put short-term investments in illiquid vehicles (like annuities) or risky securities (like internet high fliers).

IRA - This stands for "Individual Retirement Account." There are many different types of IRAs: some for small businesses

(SEP IRAs or SIMPLE IRAs) and some for individuals (Traditional IRAs and ROTH IRAs). What each of these have in common is that they are accounts that a person can put money from income into, and receive a tax benefit in return. For tax deferred accounts (Traditional IRAs, SEP IRAs, 401Ks, 403bs), money invested is then deducted from the contributor's income in the current year, so the contributor pays lower taxes in that year. Then, contributions can grow and no taxes are owed on the gains or income until distributions begin in retirement (indeed there are penalties if a person tries to take money out of a retirement account before age 59.5). When distributions occur in retirement, the account owner will have to add the distributions to their income, and pay income taxes on the total amount. ROTH IRAs are different in that contributions are made with after tax dollars, so there is no tax break in the year of the contribution. And, no taxes are owed when the account owner goes to take distributions in retirement. In summary, for a Traditional IRA, taxes are *deferred* until retirement. For a ROTH IRA, distributions in retirement are tax *free*.

Junk Bonds - These are low-grade fixed income investments. The rating agencies (see high grade definition above) assign a low rating to bonds from companies or agencies that are experiencing financial trouble. Since the term "junk bonds" has such a negative ring to it, Wall Street came up with the euphemism "high yield" to use instead. Junk bonds are called high yield bonds. These bonds need to offer a higher yield in order to entice investors to take on the higher level of risk. But, there can be a place for high yield/junk bonds in a fixed income portfolio. A small portion of high yield bonds provide a little extra income to an otherwise conservative portfolio. High yield means higher risk, but not definite risk. So adding this to a portfolio is a step that can be taken, but only with careful planning and expectations.

Leverage - In finance terms, this means exactly the same as debt or a loan. Credit also means the same thing. A credit card is a debt card...but they'd never get us to use them if we thought of them that way, now would they?

Liquidity - This refers to how easy it is to turn an investment into cash. Think of a spectrum. Some things that are really easy to turn into cash (like, well, cash) are highly liquid investments. Stocks and bonds and mutual funds are very liquid too, not quite as liquid as cash, but close. Just one call to your (super honest, open-minded, and attentive) broker and your holdings are turned into cash...for a small commission. Other assets are not liquid, or are less liquid. Real estate or part ownership in your brother's pizza shop are very illiquid assets. If you need cash tomorrow, try selling that 10% share of your brother's business, or that condo that's been on the market for almost a year.

Money Market Funds - These are technically mutual funds that contain highly liquid and safe investments. Money market funds comprise the cash portion of a brokerage account's asset allocation. They are composed of very short-term "near cash" investments, such as short-term CDs or bank notes. Typically, any cash that is uninvested in an investor's brokerage account is automatically swept into money market funds. They provide a safe place to park cash for a time, and a low rate of return. In 2009, even money market funds showed that during a collapse, nothing is completely safe. There were some money market funds that famously had to receive contributions from their parent companies to keep from "breaking the buck" or going negative. This had been unimaginable a few months prior.

Mortgages, Fixed Rate - Most people don't have enough cash laying around that they can buy a house outright, so they put some money down (hopefully more than 20%) and borrow the rest. The money they borrow is called a mortgage. In a fixed rate mortgage, the rate of interest you pay to the lender never changes, throughout the length (or term) of the loan (or mortgage). For example, if you had a 30 year, fixed rate mortgage, your interest rate wouldn't change on that mortgage for 30 years. This can be helpful in terms of planning, because you'll know exactly what you owe, each month, for thirty years. You can pay mortgages off early, but if you don't, you know what you'll owe. Typical terms for fixed rate mortgages are 15, 20, and 30 years.

Mortgages, Variable Rate - Like the definition above, except in this case the interest rate can change over the life of the loan. For example, some variable rate mortgages have a super duper low rate which doesn't changed for a certain period, like 5 years. Then, once that 5 years is up, the rate is adjusted. Upwards. Becoming much more expensive. These types of mortgages can be good if you were only planning to own a certain property for a couple of years (some people move a lot). But if you were planning to live in a certain property for many years, think hard about the adjusting rate feature before signing on for a variable rate mortgage. It might be a fit for you, but then again, it might not.

Mutual Fund - This is an investment that you can put money into if you want an easy way to diversify your investment. Basically, if you have say $1000 to invest, it might be hard for you to diversify that investment...it'd be difficult to buy shares in 100 different companies with your one grand. Mutual funds do this for you. They take your one thousand dollars and pool it with many other investors, then with that larger pool of cash, they invest into a diversified portfolio. There are many types of mutual funds, from aggressive to conservative, from cheap index funds (which are only supposed to mirror the performance of a certain index, like the S&P 500) to actively managed funds (which, for a fee, employ supposedly smart people to make active trades in the fund in an effort to provide performance that is better than an index). Which fund is for you is a matter of preference and depends upon things like your age, how much risk you want, how sensitive you are to volatility and fees, etc.

Net Income - As on the Income Statement or income and expense worksheet, net income is the income that's remaining after all expenses are subtracted. Corporations pay taxes on net income, that is income after cash and non-cash expenses. Individuals pay taxes on taxable income, which is similar: income minus deductions.

Net Worth Statement - Essentially the same thing as the Balance Sheet described above. The Balance Sheet is the term used more commonly for an organization and Net Worth Statement is used for an individual or very small organization.

Principal - This is the amount of an outstanding loan that has not yet been paid off. Does not include interest.

Retirement Plan - There are many different types of retirement plans, but in essence, a retirement plan is something your employer has put in place that you can use to save for retirement. Different types include the 401(k), 403(b), pension plans, and so on. They typically have a lot of rules and guidelines, laid out by the government to protect participants (you) from employers that might seek sneaky ways to stash away money without paying taxes (not that that would *ever* happen). For participants (employees), these plans are generally a good thing. If you sign up to participate, and you should, your contributions are normally taken about of your paycheck and sent directly to your account at the plan. Also, you are sometimes given a match, which means that your employer puts away a certain amount into your account on your behalf (it's like getting a bonus: if you put away money— they put away some too). Retirement plans are an effective way to make sure you're saving money for your future. And if you ever leave your job, your retirement plan account is still yours. You can roll it into an IRA or transfer it into the plan of your next employer. There are a few more wrinkles and bells and whistles about retirement plans, but for now, that about explains them.

Rolling Grants Cycle - Sometimes, grant applications (especially for smallish grants) are accepted, reviewed, and approved throughout the year, without a specific deadline in place. This means, if you were applying for a grant with a rolling application cycle, you could apply any time during the year. Even still, it would probably make sense to understand if there is a better or worse time throughout the year to try to tap into this process. For example, you might not want to submit right before the holidays or their major grant deadline.

Sales Load - The term used to describe an expense charged to you when you buy certain mutual funds. There are many different share classes of mutual funds, and so there are many different sales loads. The term "sales load" sounds pretty negative, right? And sometimes, you might really be better off not using a fund that charges a sales load. But, this isn't the only criteria you should use in assessing a fund. If the fund is an excellent performer, seems it will do just what you need in a fund, has a long track record, and so on, it might be worth the fee to buy into it. Or it might not. Do some homework, make a decision based on several factors. Don't just look at this one factor. Index funds do not have sales loads, so are appealing to many people because they are cheaper. Generally, for large cap equity funds, you'd be better off with an index fund because few managers in this style can beat their index over a long period of time. But, with other styles on investing (foreign, small cap, high yield, etc.), active fund managers can often beat their index. So, maybe the best thing is to use a blend of index and active funds.

Self-Employment Income - Earnings from a sole proprietor's business, net of expenses.

Short Sale - When a the price of a home is "underwater" or, the value of the home is less that the mortgage held by the homeowner, the short sale can be the only way out. A short sale is a negotiated settlement between a homeowner and their lender. There are many resources a person could turn to in order to learn about short sales. The FDIC, Freddie Mac, Fannie Mae, and state housing agencies all have educational resources available. Also, banks often provide resources, but be careful because banks are in the business of selling mortgages and other financial services. You have to understand that just about everyone in the financial services world is marketing themselves in one way or another, so be aware.

Sometimes, especially during the housing crisis that began in 2007 or so, borrowers can get over their heads with their debt obligations and become simply unable to pay back their loans. A short sale can be a way out of this mess. The lender or bank will be willing to consider a short sale application only as a last resort before foreclosure.

For a lender, a short sale is making the best of a bad situation: either the lender accepts a short sale, or the homeowner completely walks away from the mortgage (that is, stops paying, permanently) and the bank is stuck owning a vacant house. The short sale can be a slightly better (though still bad) solution.

So if this unhappy situation arises, the borrower (homeowner) may contact the lender and explain how they just cannot afford to pay anymore. The lender may decide to begin the short sale application process:

Sole Proprietor - You are the sole owner of a business that is not incorporated. For example, a self-employed artist.

Stock - A stock is a part ownership in a company. Every company has a certain monetary value (or, each company is worth a certain amount of money). Say you figured out the value of a company. Divide this value into a number of equal parts (say a thousand parts, or a million). Then these parts, called "shares," can be sold to investors. Each investor becomes part owner of the company, according to the number of shares they bought. The company can use the proceeds from selling those shares to fund their business operations. Private companies sell shares to a small circle of investors. Public companies sell shares on open markets, called exchanges (such as the New York Stock Exchange or NASDAQ, there are many exchanges in the United States and abroad). Once the company has sold (or "issued") shares to the public via an exchange, the shares are then traded among people based on whether an investor wants to hold or sell their shares. After a public company originally issues its shares on an exchange and has received proceeds from that action (called an offering, like an initial public offering or "IPO"), it doesn't receive any additional money when one investor sells its shares to another.

Submission Guidelines - These are the "how to" instructions that grant making organizations publicize so that potential applicants can know whether to submit an application and how. They are usually very carefully worded and provide everything you could reasonably want to know about whether you should pursue a grant from a certain organization. They are a vital source of information. Many applicants ignore them. Or only give them a quick read...which results in? That's right, rejection. Read the submission guidelines, first.

Tax Preparer - Come tax season, many people prepare taxes for other people or companies, for a fee. You don't have to have a certified public accountant or "CPA" designation to prepare taxes. Many people work as self-employed tax preparers and use software or their own experience or both to help people get their taxes done. They have a crazy busy season from January through April, and then close down shop and go back to their other lives as artists or fishermen or vagrants or whatever.

Transunion, Equifax, and Experion - The three major US credit bureaus. The Fair Isaac Corporation uses this info to create a number that lenders (such as banks, credit card issuers and the like) use to evaluate your credit risk. This score is called your FICO score.

Universal Default - A unpopular and relatively little known tactic in the consumer lending industry during the 1990s and early 2000s. Under this widespread practice, a consumer's behavior in one credit contract could be used to change terms in all other areas. For example, if a consumer defaulted or became otherwise delinquent in one contract (say, a department store card), then issuers for all the other credit cards owned by that consumer could respond. Responses included greatly raised rates, fees, even cancellation. This was very unpopular due to its seeming insidiousness. Also, consumers rarely received obvious notice from issuers that their rates were being changed (no phone calls, just higher expenses). After much lobbying and complaint, this practice was largely curtailed through the Credit Card Accountability and Disclosure Act of 2009, or the Credit CARD Act. Of course, not all elements of universal default were repealed. Issuers can still cancel your card if you default in another area of your financial life...so read the fine print, and make phone calls.

W-2 - The tax form employees receive annually, showing earnings and withholdings. Brought to accountant or hidden in drawer.

1099 - Statement of annual earnings for a sole proprietor, copy goes to the IRS.

401k - The 401k is a retirement plan arrangement that was developed by the IRS to encourage Americans to save their own money for their own retirement. Conceptually, these plans really favor the individual account owner and can be a very good thing. Plans are sponsored (or set up) by an employer for employees. Each employee who wants to participate (i.e., become a "participant," clever, huh?) can open an account in the 401k plan. They can contribute a certain amount from their periodic pay into their 401k account. Within their account, they can usually invest in a variety of different mutual funds, sometimes also in company stock.

Contributions that are made by the employee are tax deductible. So, say an employee pays taxes on $30,000 income per year. If they contribute $3,000 to their 401k plan, then they'd reduce the amount of taxable income by the amount of their contribution, to $27,000. There are limits to how much an employee can contribute per year, but those limits are relatively high, like $16,500 per person for 2011.

The contributions grow and cannot be accessed (without penalty) until the account owner reaches the age of 59.5 (why the half year? Ask congress). Some time after that age is reached, when the account owner starts to take distributions, they will pay income taxes on what they take out, at their then current tax rate. If they wait until they are 70.5 before taking distributions, the IRS will make them begin to take required distributions each year. The amount of the required distribution is governed by a table published by the IRS each year.

If someone takes money out of their retirement account (be it a 401k, 403b, Traditional IRA, SEP IRA, or other tax deferred plan) they will have to pay income taxes on the amount of the distribution, plus they'll pay a 10% penalty. So, for every dollar withdrawn before age 59.5, a person could end up only seeing 65% of that.

COLLABORATORS & CONTRIBUTORS

Phoebe Bean - Phoebe is a librarian at the Rhode Island Historical Society and is President of the Rhode Island Center for the Book. She holds a BA in Religious Studies from Brown University and a Masters of Library and Information Science from the University or Rhode Island. She served as proofreader for this book.

Allison Boesch - Allison was, at the time of her contribution, a junior at the Rhode Island School of Design. She's gone on to graduate and do great things. At RISD she studied illustration. She illustrated the chapter about the artist co-op.

Jim Bush - Jim is an artist and political cartoonist for the Providence Journal in Providence, RI. His studio is located in Warren, RI and is open by appointment. He lives in Providence, RI with his wife, three children, and dog Maggie. He has a piece up now at The Connecticut Academy of Fine Arts, 98th Annual Exhibit. His most recent award is Honorable Mention in The Art League of Rhode Island's annual member's exhibition ongoing right now at <u>Gallery 297</u> in Bristol, RI. He illustrated the chapter about mortgages and getting organized.

Elizabeth Cole Sheehan - Liz is an artist studying dress and costume; clothing is her medium. Sheehan is currently interested in further developing her apparel/textiles practice for the purpose of teaching and creative work. Expanding her visual vocabulary, and the ways in which she may communicate ideas, Sheehan is exploring our human connection to textiles, fashion and design, enabling her to assist others on their art journey. With her community-engaged creative practice

Sheehan chooses to investigate questions, solve problems and make meaning in dialogue with community. Creating illustrations for this project is another way to make connections. She illustrated the chapter where Prudence confronted debt.

Jeff Cooperman - Jeff has been an animator in the Bay Area for the past 10 years, working for studios such as Lucas Arts, Sega and Activision and is currently developing the next Skylanders. He also teaches character animation at the Academy of Art University. Prior to his career in animation, he worked as an art director and illustrator in the advertising world of New York. Jeff received his MBA from the New York Academy of Art and BA from Kenyon College. When he isn't working or teaching, he spends his time with his four kids and incredible wife, Catharyn. He illustrated the chapter on getting a grant.

Anna Rosenfeld - At the time of her contribution, Anna was a junior at the Rhode Island School of Design, majoring in Illustration (as if we couldn't tell!). She illustrated the chapter where Art gets in trouble with his taxes.

Richard Streitfeld - Rich is a CPA (and, like in the case, isn't it kinda funny to have a an accountant named "Rich?"). He loves working with entrepreneurs and other creative types. Nicknamed "Buddhist mensch accountant", he did seven years of hard labor directing an international Buddhist organization. Having achieved bliss, he then turned to accounting. He is a partner with Aaronson Lavoie Streitfeld Diaz and Co., P.C. in Rhode Island. They put up with his antics because he does good work and is a fine fellow. He is also a Certified Fraud Examiner. He served as tax expert, consulting on the chapter where Art confronted his fear of taxes.

Ivy Tai - Ivy was a senior at Rhode Island School of Design when she made her contribution. She majored in illustration. She illustrated the chapter about financial statements.

Rhode Island State Council on the Arts (RISCA) - Many many thanks to the awesome and amazing Cristina DiChiera and the rest of the gang at RISCA. They are an integral and vital part of the arts scene in Rhode Island, an agency that makes things happen for individual artists. Reach them at (401) 222-3880, or visit their website www.arts.ri.gov to learn more. Cristina's advice and support throughout the development of this work, both in print and online, was spot on and crucial.

RISD's Center for Student Involvement - They help students. A lot. And they want to do even more! Call them! 401-454-6607. They Rock! This group provided great support and insight into the way artists view financial planning. Their offices served as a sort of incubator for this project. Many thanks to them all, especially to the selfless work of Don Morton.

Peace, Love, and Financial Planning

Made in the USA
Lexington, KY
14 December 2012